ESSENTIAL
ALFA ROMEO
GIULIA & GIULIETTA
COUPES & SPIDERS

ESSENTIAL
ALFA ROMEO
GIULIA & GIULIETTA
COUPES & SPIDERS

THE CARS AND THEIR STORY
1954-95

DAVID HODGES

SPECIAL PHOTOGRAPHY BY ANTONIO MAFFEIS

BAY VIEW BOOKS

Published 1995 by Bay View Books Ltd
The Red House, 25-26 Bridgeland Street,
Bideford, Devon EX39 2PZ

© Copyright 1995 by Bay View Books Ltd
Edited by Mark Hughes
Typesetting and design by Chris Fayers & Sarah Ward

ISBN 1 870979 59 1
Printed in Hong Kong

CONTENTS

CHANGING TIMES

One of the great sporting marques, Alfa Romeo was committed to a drive towards mass production in the years following the Second World War and this led to a succession of models with characteristics that set them apart for most enthusiastic drivers, some of them in the tradition of the great Alfa sports cars of the 1920s and 1930s. The ranges have sometimes included fairly unsuccessful models, strategies have been uncertain in times of business stress, and racing fortunes have been mixed. But for almost half a century the bread-and-butter cars have been complemented by more sporting models, with the cars that are the subject of this book built in one form or another for 40 years. They have contributed mightily to the lustre that surrounds Alfa Romeo's name.

Alfa Romeo is one of the venerated marques of the European industry. The first ALFA cars appeared in

Alfa Romeo's large stand at the Turin Motor Show awaits the finishing touches late in May 1954, and then the hordes anxious to see the new small model in coupé form. That Giulietta Sprint naturally has a prominent position, and a long banner above the stand proclaims its qualities – sporting, aerodynamic, interior space, nimble handling and 160kph top speed.

1910, and the Alfa Romeo name was adopted after the First World War, as Nicola Romeo had taken on the company in 1915 when a bank had sent in the receivers. Romeo was an enthusiast, and that was reflected almost immediately, in Merosi's post-war designs. However, the touch of magic that set the marque apart is to the credit of Vittorio Jano, and his cars: the Grand Prix P2 that Romeo's intermediary Enzo Ferrari had enticed him

The twin-cam engine was outstanding on its 1954 launch, and still an excellent engine three decades later. From the Giulietta Sprint to the most recent Spider, it is a common thread through this book.

away from Fiat to design, the supreme six- and eight-cylinder sports cars, and the monoposto Tipo B. Without exception they were outstanding, on the Grand Prix circuits bowing only to the technological bludgeoning of well-resourced German teams in the 1930s, but unsurpassed in artistry.

That distinction was to endure, and as the 1990s opened there were more than 150 Alfa Romeo enthusiasts' clubs in 30 countries, some small and precious (such as the GTZ Register), some large national organisations. Many of their members have been attracted to the marque by the sporting qualities of the first Alfa Romeo small cars discussed in this book.

Alfa's future in the automobile industry was uncertain after the Second World War. Although a glorious reputation had been established for racing and high-performance road cars, state policy from the late 1930s meant a legacy of marginalised car production. While a few cars were built during the war to uphold national prestige, the company concentrated on trucks and aircraft engines, and this was one very good reason for the devastating air raids on its Portello factory in 1943-44. Cars trickled out through the early 1940s, including the 6C 2500 that had been the herald of an intended return to car production in some numbers.

Existing components were used to complete three cars in 1946, before proper production of the 6C 2500 was resumed in 1947. Immediate company survival, meanwhile, had depended on making household items such as cookers and window blinds. The Finmeccanica holding company, through the IRI government agency, was largely responsible for the company's rejuvenation, while factory reconstruction depended to a degree on the Marshall Plan funds that were distributed to rebuild the economies of the defeated nations. Incidentally, this financial aid might have been jeopardised when Alfa Romeo returned to Grand Prix racing with the pre-war 158s that had fortuitously been evacuated in 1943 from Monza to the village of Melzo, where the Experimental Department found safe haven in the foothills of the Alps. Grand Prix racing could have been seen by the Marshall Plan donors as a frivolous misapplication, but there were assurances that the team's funding was independent and in any case the team was withdraw in 1949 when the design of the 1900 was finalised.

The first post-war programme for reviving car production was laid down under Pasqualo Gallo, the company president, and Giuseppe Luraghi, the Finmeccanica director responsible for Alfa Romeo affairs who was destined to become Alfa's president. Their plans were executed by Director of Projects Orazio Satta Puliga.

Dott Ing Puliga, usually known as Satta, was born in 1910, and qualified in mechanical and aeronautical engineering. He joined Alfa Romeo in 1938 to work under Wilfredo Ricart, and in 1946 was appointed projects director, with the responsibility of taking the company into the new age of volume production as well as for the new models. While Bruno Trevisan and Wilfredo Ricart briefly filled the chief designer role, Satta was the natural successor to the great Vittorio Jano, Alfa's true design genius before the war. Immediately, he was responsible for both the post-war 6Cs and for the 1900.

The 1900 was Alfa Romeo's first unitary construction model, and the first intended for mass production. It was an important car in that it established, in its monocoque and four-cylinder engine, the mechanical pattern that would be followed in the Giulietta and the Giulia, as well as marketing intentions. It marked a decisive shift away from Alfa's exclusive high-performance car policy, and the occasional moves back to that type of car over the next 25 years only served to endorse this strategy.

Alfa Romeo was becoming a healthy company as 1900s started to go out of the showrooms, but to utilise the capacity fully at the Portello factory a range of smaller models was called for. This could have meant competing with Fiat, but Satta avoided a direct confrontation by deciding on a 1.3-litre engine capacity for the 750 project, that became Giulietta. There were Fiats, and others, with both smaller and larger engines than this, but nothing significant at this size, and certainly none with such an efficient engine…

Romeo and Juliet. Romeo van (in background) and Giulietta during the Portello presentation, with tiny hitches. Someone tied that floral garland across a door that was to be opened…

The sporting Alfa Romeo family in 1957 – from left are 1900 coupé, Giulietta Spider and Giulietta Sprint. The ancient setting chosen by this essentially Milanese marque is in Milan.

Prominent Alfa Romeo men of the 1960s. From left are Orazio Satta Puliga, Giuseppe Busso, company president Giuseppe Luraghi and the unmistakable figure of Carlo Chiti of Autodelta.

The 1900 saloon first shown in May 1950 had prosaic but efficient lines, and its 1884cc twin-cam engine rated at 90bhp gave it a rounded, and impressive, maximum speed of 150kph. Had Alfa worked in Imperial measures the claim might have been 95mph, but that 150kph accurately converts to 93mph. This engine was advanced among contemporary production units, having a cast iron block and alloy cylinder heads with large combustion chambers, generous gas flow and twin overhead camshafts driven by roller chains, operating the valves through inverted piston-type tappets. It was the basis of the smaller, lighter and even more efficient engine that was to be developed for the Giulietta. Once production had settled down, a 1900 TI was introduced in 1951 with a 100bhp engine giving a 170kph (106mph) top speed. Expensive Farina and Touring cabriolet and coupé versions soon followed, then there was a Tulip Rally victory, and prejudices against Alfa Romeos with mere four-cylinder engines were largely overcome.

There were also 'Super' versions with slightly larger engines, having 1975cc from 1953, and more coachbuilt coupés and spiders, some shapely and some odd. The larger cars continued into the 1960s, with six-cylinder 2600 derivatives following from 1962 until the end of the decade. As the Grand Prix programme with the all-conquering 158/159 ended, there was also some competition work with the 1900. However, the Disco Volante/6C 3000M episode in 1953 delivered little, in part because of management schisms in the background – the decision to go ahead with this programme had not been unanimous.

Meanwhile, the smaller model which was intended to widen Alfa Romeo's market penetration was gradually taking shape, and it was to provide the basis for sound competition cars. The Giulietta would be smaller than the 1900 in its principal dimensions, and lighter too. The engine was essentially a 1290cc version of the twin-cam straight four with a light alloy block, at a time when such advanced construction was rare in production saloons. In its saloon version, the Giulietta was much cheaper than the 1900, and once production got under way it was built in much larger numbers, becoming the first Alfa to have five-figure annual production figures. It was the mainstay of the company's sales as the 1950s gave way to the 1960s.

The limited-production Freccia d'Oro in the post-war 2500 range was the first Alfa to be named, and Giulietta was the second. At the 1954 Turin Motor Show the coupé was welcomed as 'a true Alfa Romeo', and given pride of place in reports. The saloon was unveiled

These coupés maintained Alfa's tradition of sporting success, most notably in the second half of the 1960s. GTAs overwhelm the Porsches in this 1967 Nürburgring Six Hours group.

later, with an appropriately Shakespearian flourish at the Portello factory, where an actress in costume introduced 'Juliet', or 'Giulietta'. A Romeo accompanied her, for a van carrying that name was announced at the same time. The 1290cc twin-cam engine must have made for quick deliveries, and there was also an alternative 1158cc supercharged twin-cylinder proprietary diesel, although this sounds most unlike Alfa Romeo.

Charismatic line ....

In an odd reversal of normal motor industry practice the 'performance' Giulietta came before the saloon, largely because late completion of the body plant led to an embarrassing situation. The public had been induced to

An immaculate right-hand drive Giulietta Sprint. Giuliettas received this style of mesh trim for their side grilles in 1959.

Three decades are represented here, in a red 2000 GTV, a white Sprint GT and a late 'square-tail' spider.

invest in Alfa Romeo factory modernisation and tooling with the lure that 200 of the debenture holders would win a new Giulietta saloon. This model failed to make its expected 1953 debut and still did not appear at the 1954 Geneva Motor Show, but by that stage the mechanical elements could be produced, and an in-house sports coupé proposal suggested that limited production by one of the specialist coachbuilders was possible. A run of a thousand was projected, with 200 going to the prize-winners and thereby stifling a growing scandal. This Giulietta Sprint was unveiled at the 1954 Turin Motor Show, and the new model received such a positive response that orders approaching 3000 were reported by the end of the show…

Carrozzeria Bertone built these Giulietta Sprints, getting the car into production quickly by developing an existing coupé design designated Project 37. Bertone also had a reputation for low production costs because, unlike most coachbuilders, its bodies took shape on jigs without the mechanical and chassis elements of the car, so it was the ideal choice for the commission. Like Alfa Romeo, Bertone had survived a difficult post-war phase. A run of Arnolt-MGs was an important factor in Bertone's recovery, and the famous Franco Scaglione-designed BAT (Berlina Aerodinamica Tecnica) cars of 1953 were important to its future, as well as being the first official liaison with Alfa Romeo.

Bertone's coupé body for the Giulietta Sprint was restrained after the flamboyance of the BAT cars and other Abarth-based extravaganzas. Free of ornamentation and distinctly sporting, it was to be enormously successful. And presumably the 200 Italian prize-winners realised that they were very lucky, although they could

hardly have known that their sports coupé was in many ways the forerunner of the hot hatch…

Bertone also built a Giulietta cabriolet, but the soft-top version of the Giulietta that eventually reached production was styled and built by Pininfarina, whose 'Spyder' affectation was to be applied to it, and is often used generically. The word, like so many coachbuilding terms, comes from the days of horse-drawn vehicles, when a spider was a light two- or four-wheel carriage, with no entymological associations. It was an English (or possibly American) term which found its automotive application in Europe, especially in Italy.

The engine, transmission and running gear of the Giulietta Spider were shared with the other models, but no body panels were carried over. The introduction came in the summer of 1955, within months of the saloon. Its positive lines (coupled with sensible features such as wind-up windows at a time when some sports car manufacturers still expected customers to accept less sophisticated arrangements), its 100mph top speed and the lure of an Alfa Romeo badge on an open sports car ensured its success.

These coupés and spiders transformed the Alfa Romeo image in the USA, which became an important market for the company. The numbers called for also led Pininfarina and Bertone into the world of quantity production.

'Veloce' versions of both Giulietta models were to come, and hotter variants, before the Giulia was introduced in 1962. The Giulietta survived a while before fading away in 1965 with the Italian 'taxation special' 1300 Sprint (a hastily-imposed extra tax in 1964 led to Alfa home sales dropping by a fifth, then that purchase tax was removed in 1965). The four-door Giulia saloons appeared distinctly boxy, but they were still aerodynamically efficient with a 0.34 Cd. They were sensible in the use of the three box spaces for machinery, people and luggage, and they were sporty. The coupé was to be the first car entirely built at the new 'green field' site plant at Arese, a few miles north-west of Milan (the old Portello factory was to be demolished).

Spider and coupé versions followed the saloon quickly. Pininfarina's open car was first, for it continued with the existing body combined with Giulia mechanical elements as the carrozzeria moved towards a new body that was to be launched as the Duetto in 1966. Alfa Romeo was to build the new coupé, but Bertone was again entrusted with the design, a commission that was deserved in view of the success of the Giulietta Sprint. Scaglione had recently left and Nuccio Bertone put the new coupé project into the hands of a young Torinese designer, Giorgio Giugiaro, who actually did the work as a part-time job during his period of national service in the army. Its styling broadly echoed the Giulietta Sprint, but it was more svelte and cohesive. Inside it was still scaled for Italians, but despite the slightly shorter wheelbase Giugiaro went some way to meet Alfa's requirement that it should be a four-seater. In reality it was a 2+2 coupé.

In the mid-1960s Touring was to produce the GTC cabriolet derivative of the coupé, and the chassis number sequences even extended to the sleek *Sprint Speciale*, the *Tubolare* competition specials and the Zagato 4R evocation of the 1930s 6C 1750. The series numbers, 750 for the first cars, then 101, 105 and 115, with sub-designations that do not seem entirely logical, are identification codes that are familiar among *Alfisti* but bewildering to others…

The next main-line Giulia development was significant, for the 1966 Spider – named Duetto soon

In Italy limited-edition and high-performance spin-offs from quality production models were always inevitable. These two are both by Zagato: the SZ (top) was derived from the Giulietta, and the Junior Z (above) from the Giulia.

after its introduction – was the last car in which Battista Pinin Farina was directly involved (although it was really a studio team effort) and it was to survive into the 1990s. Fortunately it owed little beyond detailing to a succession of Pininfarina Alfa-based two-seater show cars, although the theme of scalloped flanks was carried through to this new model. It had sleek lines that were compared less than favourably with the Giulietta Spider's, but would confound critics as they proved timeless. There were shortcomings, including the limited cockpit space that might have been acceptable in 1966 but was far less so in the 1990s, the scuttle shake that was never wholly overcome, and the fundamental flaw that even the most dedicated Alfa Romeo *aficionado* cannot deny – Pininfarina's construction almost seemed to invite

The second-generation open two-seaters had a very long life, starting with the clean-lined 1966 Duetto with its 'boat-tail' rear-end styling.

Touring Cars in the 1990s, the record of the Alfa coupés was consistently superb.

From the mid-1960s the competition cars, and the racing activities, were the responsibility of Autodelta, which started well but later became an embarrassment with its inept Formula 1 programme. A reborn Alfa Corse later restored racing pride in the marque through modern saloon car racing. Thus from the Giulietta to the 155 touring cars of 1994, the most successful Alfa circuit cars of the last four decades have had roofs…

The coupé shape lingered on in the GTVs, fading away with the 1971-77 2000 GTV, a car that still looked good even if it felt a little narrow in the cockpit by 1970s standards. The Spider continued through the 1980s, with some body add-ons that did nothing for its lines, but with a subtle bodywork redesign as the decade ended restoring attractive lines. The last Spider 2000 was built in 1993.

Through the past decade Alfa Romeo's continuing existence could never be taken for granted. In looking at one range of cars, it is easy to overlook a company's financially precarious periods, and in the case of Alfa Romeo easy to forget that a Ford association was the subject of a joint study early in 1986, before Fiat took over. At the time, and over the next five years, the end of Spider production was confidently predicted, and there was speculation about its replacement.

The Alfa SZ from 1990 picked up something of the coupé theme, but although its dramatic Alfa-styled, Zagato-built body might have been efficient in aerodynamic respects, it had little visual charm. On those grounds alone, the shapely GTV coupé and spider that arrived in 1995 are most welcome…

The earlier Alfa coupés and spiders had been sporting cars in the best Italian tradition, with few of the compromises that marketing men or accountants might have imposed on such cars in other companies. In Italy the saloons became commonplace and they were cheap, but somehow this did not undermine Alfa Romeo's cherished image, or the warm perception of the coupés and spiders outside Italy. In retrospect, of course, these cars had shortcomings, and the competition record of the spiders was slender. But they outlived most contemporary sports cars, with a lifespan matched only by the very different products of Morgan and Lotus/Caterham, or, stretching a point, the frequently updated Chevrolet Corvettes.

The British and Italian approaches had been very different, but they both owed nothing to computers and a lot to flair and feel. The Alfa Romeos were great expressions of automotive art…

rust. But in such pretty cars much can be forgiven.

Junior variants of the Giulias, with 1290cc engines, kept Alfa's market broad, but there were few of the speciality spin-offs one might have expected Italian coachbuilders to produce on such promising bases, especially as many appeared on 1900 chassis. Only the SS, Touring's GTC and Zagato's Junior Z achieved four-figure production with Giulia-based cars, while there was a mere handful of concept cars.

The Giulia Sprint GT continued through most of the 1960s, while the coupé range was extended sideways to variants intended for competition. In top-level touring car racing, the GTA, GTA Junior and GTAm were the most successful models in the Giulietta and Giulia family. Indeed, after the legendary Grand Prix 158/159, they were the most convincing Alfas in international motor racing, an evaluation that does not overlook the sports racing cars of the 1970s. From the European Touring Car and TransAm Championships in the second half of the 1960s, to the FIA European Challenge for Historic

THE GIULIETTA

The simple and effective lines of the Sprint, seen here in the 'hatchback' form used only in the first year, did not call for adornment. The reflection along the side picks up the lower level of the 'tumblehome', which shows better in the wooden buck preserved in the Alfa Romeo Museum (below).

The Giulietta was straightforward, following on from the 1900 but obviously less expensive, and not adventurous in concept – an appropriate top-drawer manufacturer's approach to a wider and increasingly international market.

The mechanical make-up – a front-mounted 1.3-litre engine driving the rear wheels through a four-speed gearbox – was common to all the body styles, so the fact that the first Giulietta to be tested by *The Motor* was a TI saloon was less significant than the reactions to the car. In those days, the magazine's technical staff were qualified men who observed standard procedures in setting down objective assessments. The 1958 report on the Giulietta TI opened:

'Any car in the under 1½-litre class which can reach 50mph from rest in less than 15sec, 70mph from rest in under 30sec, which will combine a true road speed of 85mph with a fuel consumption of, say, 27mpg, can be considered in the top class as far as acceleration, speed and fuel economy are concerned.

'When therefore it is claimed that a 1.3-litre car has reached 50mph in less than 12sec, 70mph in under 23sec, and has combined 27mpg with but a fraction under 100mph (a magic figure that can actually be exceeded in

slightly favourable conditions), the reader's reaction may well be that of incredulity. He may think that distances and instruments were in error, or if reassured on this point, that some serious sacrifices have been made such as the use of exceedingly low-drag, lightweight body construction at the expensive of longevity and comfort, or by fitting an engine so highly tuned that the peak of

The mature Sprint, with flawless 1950s proportions in three-quarter views from front and rear. The left-hand drive car has additional door mirrors, while the right-hand drive one follows a less sensible 1950s fashion with wing mirrors. Both have the standard fascia-mounted rear-view mirror. This Sprint interior is immaculate, but the mats show that the car is used. The standard steering wheel was not very sporting.

performance is only a passing phase whereas inflexibility, noise and vibration are permanent features.'

The report went on to explain that although the speedometer was wildly optimistic (14 per cent inaccurate at 90mph), the magazine's twin-stopwatch system was in fact accurate. And the report concluded by comparing this Alfa with other cars in its class: 'There are none which in speed or acceleration can approach the brilliant performance of the Giulietta TI, which can thereby claim the best combination of utility, safety and speed in the world today.'

'Today' was early 1958 and this final paragraph was remarkable for a journal not given to hyperbole in its road test reports. No wonder sporting drivers fell for these saloons and coupés.

The layout of the monocoque chassis/body was basically similar to the 1900, but in the four/five-seat saloon the larger glass areas resulting from thinner pillars showed one aspect of technological progress in five years. The overall Giulietta saloon proportions now seem tall and narrow, but this is less apparent in the Sprint, for the coupé is 6in lower, with the roofline following a nicely-judged curve to the tail. The first cars were hatchbacks with a side-hinged rear window, then in 1955 a

conventional boot was substituted. Wind tunnel work played no part in shaping Giulietta saloon or coupé bodies, but 1954 reports rightly drew attention to the low-drag lines of the Sprint.

The wishbone and coil spring front suspension, with an anti-roll bar and an adjustable front control arm on the wishbones, was conventional. So too was the live axle set-up at the rear, with coil springs, a T-bar to control tramp, stout trailing arms and wishbones that seemed positioned to subdue roll. Despite these efforts, these cars did roll considerably in energetic cornering, but this was regarded as acceptable lively behaviour. In normal motoring the ride was firm, but not so much that road surface irregularities made for passenger discomfort. The brakes (10½in by 2⅛in wide at the front, 10in by 1⅜in wide at the rear) were housed in impressive ribbed alloy drums, appropriate to their power and fade-free performance. The wheel trim was pierced to increase air circulation over the drums. ZF worm and roller steering was used. Pirelli Cinturato tyres were normal at first, and then Michelin X tyres which were best run at slightly lower pressures than the Cinturatos, but with either type the steering was light and responsive. In one of those details now long forgotten, if indeed it was ever known,

Sprint bodies ready to be wheeled to meet mechanical parts and suspension.

by modern motorists, chassis lubrication to 23 points was called for every 2000km (1250 miles).

The engine was a smaller version of the twin-cam four-cylinder unit introduced for the 1900, with a bore/stroke ratio nearer to 'square' and weight saved with a light alloy block (with wet cylinder liners) in place of the cast iron block of the earlier model. In broad characteristics it harked back to the GP and sports car engines of the 1930s, with inclined valves in cross-flow heads, and it maintained the tradition of efficiency too. An 1100cc proposition was abandoned at an early stage, and the 1290cc size gave tax advantages in Italy.

The Sprint engine, with a twin-choke Solex carburettor and compression ratio increased to 8.1:1, was rated at 65bhp, whereas the saloon engine gave 63bhp and the 1900 engine 90bhp. In the Giuliettas it revved freely, and in competition units to well above its 6000rpm limit. It was flexible, smooth and quiet, with some improvement coming in this respect as mountings were revised during production, and always with a subdued exhaust note in standard form. These were not the first Italian cars to be fitted with an electrical system that was not always satisfactory, nor the last.

Transmission was through an all-synchromesh four-speed gearbox, with a column change that was rated good, although in retrospect one might qualify this as 'good of its kind'. However, right-hand drive cars and the Sprint Veloce coupé were to have a floor-mounted change from 1958.

The cabin was well furnished with all the necessities expected in the 1950s, and there was a full set of instruments in the fascia, which was painted metal at first but later covered with black plastic. Cushions were provided for the space behind the supportive front seats, justifying a 'plus two' description, but only really making seats for children. Their removal allowed for adequate luggage space, for the boot volume was reduced by the battery and spare wheel, which was stowed horizontally. The fuel filler cap was also inside the boot lid of early coupés, and the very earliest of all had a cockpit release for the hatch. Fore and aft, the doors were large, but the high sill and low roofline combined to complicate access to those very occasional rear seats. The rear windows were front-hinged, opening for ventilation.

The interior was predominantly black, the fascia relieved only by the instruments – the three main ones were ahead of the driver – until a little 'wood' trim was introduced on the vertical surface. There was a lockable glovebox and a grab handle for the passenger. The thin-rimmed two-spoke steering wheel had an inner horn ring. Outwardly, a chrome strip between the wheel arches was broken in two places as it ran across the bottom of the door, to align it with the thin bumpers front and rear. Behind the front wheels the car's identity was confirmed with a chrome '1300' and a Bertone badge, while an Alfa badge and 'Sprint' script appeared above the rear number plate, '1300' beside it.

Early coupé prices in the Italian market were

1,735,000 lire for the Sprint and 2,050,000 lire for the Sprint Veloce. The corresponding Spiders were priced at 1,900,000 lire and 2,235,000 lire.

The first Spider

Chronologically the Spider came next, in the summer of 1955. This was a sports car by any definition, and it was to share Veloce uprating with the Sprint. This open version brought Pininfarina into the world of volume production.

While the bodywork carefully retained strong Giulietta resemblances, none of the body panels was common to the other models. It was a beautifully balanced design, open to criticism only in the detail of nose styling, shorter than the Sprint and with no pretence to offer seating for more than two. In its fittings, the cockpit hardly improved on the coupé, with an open cubby hole and grab handle ahead of the passenger. There were three sensible round instruments in front of

the driver, a central rev counter flanked by a speedometer on the right and a water temperature/oil pressure/fuel gauge on the left.

The pale grey Spider prototype in the Alfa Romeo Museum shows differences around the cockpit. This car has fixed side window frames, with fixed quarter lights and sliding sections in the main part. The soft-top was removable rather than folding, with three attachment points on the rear deck. The seat backs tipped forward and this allowed enough luggage space for a briefcase to be stowed upright. There was neither a glove compartment nor a grab handle, but the passenger did face a row of four pull-push controls, for drivers with long right arms. The three main dials ahead of the driver

Prototype and definitive Spiders. Apart from the window frames on the doors of the prototype, differences are in details such as the aggressive bumper horn embellishments on the American production car (right) and the rounded windscreen corners on the prototype (below).

Pininfarina's 'Spyder' (above left) became the standard production soft-top, but this one looks curiously unfinished without its wheel trims. Bertone's chunky little Giulietta-based spider (above right) was a one-off study and perhaps more attractive, but the addition of an adequate bumper might have spoiled the nose. US advertising from 1957 (right).

had the same functions, but were arranged with the rev counter at a higher level and in a nacelle extended towards the driver, as if to emphasise that this was the one that mattered. The gear lever looked exceptionally sturdy, but another early Spider had a column change. This museum car has no name on the rear, just an Alfa badge on the nose and Pininfarina's 'f' emblem behind the front wheel arches. Unlike the coupé, the chrome strip between the wheel arches ran below the doors and was unbroken.

The Spider scored over its popular British counterparts in sophistication, notably in its wind-up windows and its soft-top, which was easy to erect and fold, and could be tucked away under a neat cover between the seat backs and the front-hinged boot lid. Overall, as well as in its wheelbase, the Spider was shorter than the coupé, but the absence of occasional seats meant that more boot space could be provided, particularly as the spare wheel was stowed ahead of the boot.

Outwardly the nose followed coupé lines, but a divided bumper accommodated the lower central grille, and there were prominent overriders at front and rear. In a unifying touch, chrome trim was run along the flanks at bumper height, below the doors. Apart from a spine strip on the rear-hinged bonnet and Pininfarina badges behind the front wheel arches, there was no other embellishment.

Pininfarina achieved structural integrity without

extensive bracing, the open car weighed slightly less than the coupé, and generally the Spider was rigid. While there was some scuttle shake, later Spiders were to regress in this important detail.

The only authoritative road test of one of these early Spiders appeared in *Road & Track*, which in 1956 treated 'the only Spider west of the Mississippi' very carefully. It recorded a 100mph (160kph) top speed, slightly higher than the claimed 96mph, although that itself was another conversion of a rounded figure (155kph). The magazine

Spare wheel and jack stowage on the Spider released boot space for luggage, but was hardly convenient. The chances of damaging cockpit trim when swapping wheels must have been high...

The assembly lines at Portello were cramped, with two lines of trimmed Spider bodies ready for running gear. With no room to expand, Alfa moved to its current home in Arese.

was most impressed by the $2995 price, some $400 more than a Triumph TR3. However, distributor Hoffman Motors did not hold that competitive price for long, and it soon rose to $3533.

Veloce ....

In spring 1956 Veloce versions of the coupé and Spider were introduced, for some time carrying a 'Super' name in the USA, and respectively the designations 750E and

750F in the factory nomenclature. The principal change was in the uprated engine, with a 9.1:1 compression ratio and two sidedraught Weber DC03 carburettors in place of the single Solex. The power output was increased to 90bhp at 6500rpm, compared with the 'normal' 65bhp at 6100rpm, and there was a useful torque gain.

Weight was fractionally increased to 895kg (1973lb) for the coupé, and 864kg (1905lb) for the Spider. Some lightweight panels and sliding plastic windows were available for the Sprint Veloce, which was seen to have competition potential. This model lasted for only two years, but these lightweight cars accounted for most SVs raced and rallied late in the decade. In outright performance terms, both coupé and Spider had a claimed top speed of 112mph (180kph). In 1958 *Road & Track* recorded 107mph (172kph) with a Spider, using 7000rpm, and with the speedometer actually reading 125mph (201kph). It transpired that the car involved had a non-standard final drive, and 18 months later the journal achieved a 112.5mph (181kph) top speed when testing another Spider. The first car was designated 1300SV (the initials could translate to Sprint Veloce or Spider Veloce), while the car in the second test was a 'Super Spider'. The 200kph, or 125mph, speeds were also claimed in Italian published impressions. These were not true road tests, and presumably the figures were 'speedometer reading' speeds.

How did the Giulietta coupés and Spiders compete in the showrooms? They were more sophisticated than most rivals, and also quicker than most. Price comparisons can be distorted by local taxes – early Giuliettas were almost prohibitively expensive in Britain because of duties and taxes – but prices in 'neutral' Switzerland in the spring of 1958 give yardsticks in the table below. The maximum speed figures are from manufacturers, as complete coverage from reliable independent contemporary road tests is not possible:

	Price (Swiss francs)	Max speed (kph/mph)
Alfa Romeo Giulietta Sprint	15,900	160/100
Sprint Veloce	17,900	180/112
Spider	15,250	165/103
Spider Veloce	17,250	175/109
Lancia Appia Farina Coupé	18,800	143/89
Lotus Elite	19,900	190/118
MGA hard-top	12,900	155/96
Morgan Plus Four	10,400	140/87
Porsche 356A 1600 coupé	15,950	160/100
356A 1600S coupé	17,000	175/109
Simca Aronde Océane	13,500	140/87

The Giulietta Spider's two fins were a delicate styling feature at the rear (above), but the standard Italian number plate rather spoiled the effect. The twin-cam engine was reasonably accessible, although the bonnet line could hardly have been lower (left). The hard-top (facing page) in no way looked like an afterthought or add-on, and its large wrapped glass area made for good all-round visibility.

Following the introduction of the TI saloon late in the summer of 1957, the Giulietta range was overhauled in detail, primarily to facilitate higher production rates but also to reduce production costs, in order to meet demand stimulated more by the TI saloon than by the two-door variants. The changes were spread over two years, and towards the end of that period, in 1959, there was a logic-defying switch in chassis numbering from 750 series to 101 series.

There were minor body changes to suit production, and in engine manufacture there was a change from sand casting to die casting as the engineers looked ahead to the 1570cc version. Externally the 101 series Sprints had revised grilles and rear lights, with twin number plate

lights on the bumper. Ancillaries such as carburation were modified and a stronger gearbox was introduced in 1958 with Porsche ring-type synchromesh and the capacity for a fifth gear. The Spider gained a little cockpit space when there was a 2in wheelbase extension in 1959 and the soft-top and its housing were modified.

The Giulietta range sold well, especially in the USA, so right-hand drive (on the TI saloon) was not offered until 1961. A year earlier conversions by a South African company had been approved by Alfa Romeo, and from the following year right-hand drive conversions by Rudds of Worthing became more widely known, and could be applied to earlier cars. In 1961, incidentally, the UK concessionaire, Thomson and Taylor, announced modest price cuts across the range, which brought a Spider down to just below £2000.

In 1961 *The Autocar* published impressions of a Sprint Veloce with its engine enlarged to 1470cc by Jack Mount, reporting his claim of 130bhp and recording 0-50mph (0-80kph) in 7.7sec and a maximum speed of 120.2mph (193.4kph). This can be compared with the *Automobil Revue* figures for a standard Sprint which gave a 0-80kph (0-50mph) time of 9.5sec and a maximum speed of 164kph (102mph).

The saloon was continued in TI form until 1964, after the introduction of its successor, the Giulia – Spider production ended in mid-1962 and coupé production at the end of that year. However, the coupé reappeared

The cockpit of a production Giulietta Spider (top), with main instruments where they should be rather than arranged to satisfy styling whims, controls well positioned,

'Giulietta' on the boss of the unattractive steering wheel, and a reassuring little 'f' (for Farina) in the middle of the fascia. Prototype Spider has a quite different, and peculiar, layout (above).

Sprints soon appeared in races. Preparation of this car in the 1955 Tour of Sicily (above left), a Mille Miglia style road race, seems to comprise the addition of two spot lights and removal of wheel trims. The car hurrying through a typical landscape in the 1956 Dolomites Cup (above right) typifies Italian motor sport of the period – it has bumpers and wheel trims removed. The Sprint driven by Ubezzi and Catulle at Le Mans in 1958 (left) follows the class-winning Osca out of Mulsanne Corner – the Alfa retired during the night with fuel system problems.

early in 1964 for the Italian market, where taxation was based on engine capacity. It was modified, notably in having the disc front brakes of the Giulia Sprint and instruments from the SS. It was designated '1300 Sprint' – without the Giulia name – and was offered until 1965.

Coachbuilders might have been expected to take advantage of the Giulietta more than they did. Pininfarina produced several 'exploratory' cars in the late 1950s, such as the two Superflow show models that were too adventurous or too extreme, and the Spider Sport in both open and coupé forms. Working towards the Giulia Spider, or Duetto, Pininfarina showed an intriguing hard-

top variant at Geneva in 1962. Its stainless steel roof was hinged at the rear and spring-loaded to rise a few inches above the windscreen frame for easier access.

The Giulietta did more to change perceptions of Alfa Romeo than the larger contemporary models – 1900, 2000 and 2600. The production total reached 176,580, and among this number were more Spiders than Alfa's total output of open sports cars in the 1920s and 1930s. The majority of Giulietta variants sold were Sprints – 24,084 against 14,300 Spiders, while the Sprint Veloce accounted for 3058 and the Spider Veloce for 2907. Just over half were in the 101 chassis number series. The

This trio in the 1957 Tour de Corse have French and Swiss crews. The rallying exploits of Alfas, set with the 1900, extended through to the years of the GTAs.

Spiders were not so common in competition. This Sebring 12 Hours entry in 1960 (right) has a substantial roll-over bar and appears to be at the centre of an unhurried 'worry' session in practice. On the other hand, the Greek-crewed Spider on its way to fourth place in the 1959 Acropolis Rally (below right) is definitely being hurried along.

Giulietta name was to be revived between 1977–85, for a four-door saloon with engines in three capacities.

Sprint and Spider in competition.................

In the 1300cc GT class the coupés were sufficiently competitive through the second half of the 1950s to whet Alfa Romeo sporting appetites, and they were widely used by amateurs into the 1960s. They were common in the last Mille Miglia races, and no fewer than 54 assorted Giuliettas ran in the last true Mille Miglia, in 1957. It is surprising to find only 10 in the top 130 finishers in

1955: Buttichi was 32nd overall and third in his class, where other Alfas were 4-5-6, and there was an 11th place for a Sprint Veloce in 1956. In the Targa Florio Colin Davis and 'Sepe' drove the latter's Conrero-prepared car to sixth overall and a class win in 1959, when there were four more Giuliettas among the top 20 finishers. There were 1300cc GT class wins in the Targa Florio from 1957 through to 1963, with four more top ten placings in those years.

Overall, TI saloons were more prominent in rallies, but Sprints, especially the Sprint Veloce and later the lightweight Sprint Veloce, were used with some success at international level. In 1956 Collange and Huguet won the Alpine Rally, Schell and Vidilles drove one to sixth place in the Tour de France in formidable Ferrari/Mercedes/Porsche company, and there were class wins in events such as the Dolomite Cup. Nicol and de Lageneste won the Tour de Corse in 1957, when there was also a class win in the Acropolis. Mmes M. Blanchaud and R. Wagner won the Coupe des Dames in the 1958 Monte Carlo Rally in a Sprint (a TI was second overall). That year, 1958, was a good one for Alfas in major rallies, more often saloons but sometimes TZs (which are

Spider's neat proportions and windscreen curvature displayed. There was space behind the seats for a couple of tennis racquets, but not much more. The combined badge and boot lock (left) is typical of the clever detailing to be expected of Pininfarina.

covered in the next chapter). The coupés and saloons were natural tools for the Italian rally fraternity, and as late as 1963 half of the top 20 cars in the Sardinian Rally were Giuliettas.

The appropriate field for Spiders was in amateur racing, more so in the USA than in Europe, although an American pair mixing it with the big boys were placed 18th and 19th at Sebring in 1960. Spiders were also rallied, again by amateurs and usually with claustrophobic hard-tops, and a fourth overall in the 1959 Acropolis Rally was a great result for Spider crew Michos and Theodoracopoulo.

SPECIAL VERSIONS

The balanced qualities of the Giulietta meant that special versions inevitably followed the Sprint and Spider, some with *gran turismo* potential, some with real competition potential. Bertone created a spider that looked more pugnacious than Pininfarina's production car, but it proved to be a dead-end project. At the 1958 Turin Show, Abarth exhibited a stubby space-frame coupé using Giulietta components. Carlo Abarth had collaborated in the 1955 Alfa Romeo Tipo 750 Competizione, a 1.5-litre sports-racing car with some Giulietta parts and a Boano body which did not get beyond the first tests stage but survives in Alfa Romeo's

Giulietta SS and Giulia SS were outwardly identical, save in detail, the important improvements in the later car being the larger engine and front disc brakes – this is a 1963 Giulia SS.

museum. Most significantly, that 1958 Turin Show also saw the announcement that the Sprint Speciale (or SS) coupé, which was based on the Giulietta's platform and running gear, would be built in limited numbers.

The first SS, in 1957, had been a lightweight special with a space-frame chassis and aluminium bodywork, designed by Franco Scaglione. It had some of the impractical touches that often feature on show cars, such as a highly vulnerable nose and a roof that was really too low, however much it might have contributed to a low frontal area and to aerodynamic efficiency in a car with a Cd of 0.30. Bertone's production SS was redesigned and became more practical, although some details had to be changed after a handful had been completed: a front bumper was added, although this appeared no more substantial than the vestigial rear bumper, and the headlights were raised a little to meet US requirements.

In build quality the SS was not a 'special' that showed off rippling panels and poor shut lines, but then the Italian price was some 50 per cent higher than a Sprint. The early SS had a main structure in steel, with aluminium doors, bonnet and boot lid, but on the definitive production version all bodywork except for the boot lid was in steel, and so the SS was a little heavier than the Sprint.

The engine was further uprated for this model, primarily in valve modifications, to give 100bhp at 6500rpm. This gave a claimed top speed of 200kph (roughly 125mph), outstanding for a 1.3-litre car at the end of the 1950s, even one with such slippery lines.

The Porsche-type all-synchromesh five-speed gearbox had a conventional pattern, with first and second nearest the driver in the left seat, fifth and reverse furthest from him. The suspension was carried over from the Giulietta, and despite its low build the SS inherited family roll characteristics.

The interior layout resembled the Sprint in details such as the instruments, but there was a nicer three-spoke steering wheel. The seats were reasonably supportive and the pedals (a pendant accelerator, floor-mounted clutch and brake) were well-placed for a driver of average stature, although this was a cramping car for a tall person. Visibility through the steeply raked and curving windscreen was good in normal conditions. The car's increased length resulted in greater overhangs front and rear, but boot space was niggardly, with little room even for soft bags, which still had to share the space with a spare wheel, battery and fuel filler. However, there was more space where child-size rear seats were provided, realistically allowing room for one child or a reasonable amount of luggage.

The Giulietta SS was a modest success with 1366 built, and in 1963 it was superseded by a version with the 1570cc engine used in the Giulia and rated at 112bhp. There were detail revisions, the interior was restyled, and discs took the place of the Giulia-type three leading shoe front brakes on all but the earliest cars. Late in 1964 a

The prototype Giulietta Sprint Speciale shown at the 1957 Turin Motor Show was Scaglione's lightweight coupé (above), with smooth lines that make the claimed impressive 0.30 Cd figure quite credible. Its nose was very pretty, but without the shield it did not relate to other Giulietta models, and how would it have looked with a bumper? This SS at Sebring in 1961 (below) shows the definitive nose and the slightly corpulent plan form. A second occupant could perhaps have been squeezed in by the driver.

right-hand drive version was introduced. The last SS was priced at SF 18,900 in 'neutral' Switzerland, compared with SF 21,500 for the Giulietta version in 1958.

Confusingly, these second series cars, badged '1600 SS', became part of the Giulia family, while the 1.3-litre Giulietta saloon and Sprint continued in production until 1965. The Giulia SS ran from 1963 until 1965, with the last one of the 1400 built leaving the factory in 1966. Alfa

Giulietta SS and Giulia SS. The Giulietta (above) is a 1959 car, here driven by arch-enthusiast Jon Dooley at Donington 21 years later. The Giulia SS **shows the family trait of lifting an inside wheel in energetic cornering (below), and is being raced by one M. Benchaya at Marrakesh in 1967.**

Romeo's 121mph (195kph) maximum speed figure for the second series cars was fractionally lower, and this difference was largely borne out by road tests in *Road & Track* and *The Motor*, although some of the findings are difficult to reconcile with respective 1290cc and 1570cc engines and kerb weights of 957kg (2110lb) for the early 1961 Giulietta SS and 996kg (2195lb) for the early 1965 Giulia 1600 SS.

	Max speed	0-60 mph	Standing ¼-mile
Road & Track (Giulietta SS)	120mph/193kph	12.3sec	18.4sec
The Motor (Giulia SS)	113mph/182kph	10.8sec	18.0sec

The American testers respected a privately-owned car, and had perhaps quoted the importer's top speed figure or believed the usual optimistic speedometer. *The Motor* tested a relatively low-mileage car supplied by Alfa Romeo (GB), which would probably have become quicker when it loosened up. Opinions varied: 'Wind noise is low, which we expected, but engine noise is extremely low' (*Road & Track*), or 'intake swallowing noises become intrusive to a tiring degree when driving hard' (*The Motor*). While *Road & Track* remarked on the vice-free road behaviour of the Giulietta series, *The Motor* was specific to the SS, commenting that on Pirelli Cinturato HS tyres the car 'became very tricky on wet roads' while the high roll angles and large suspension movements led to bump steering and the car's inclination to 'float off course at each disturbance, requiring tiring concentration at speeds over 75mph, except on reasonably flat surfaces'.

Meanwhile, a Zagato special with a lower and smoother body led to the limited-production Giulietta SZ (Sprint Zagato). This was a no-nonsense competition car; the 210 built ensured homologation, although there were to be scrutineering quibbles about disc brakes. In 1959 an Alfa Romeo contract for these cars signalled the company's intention to return to serious motor sport, and the same year the company took the next step by initiating work on the GTZ.

The first Zagato special was built on the chassis of a Sprint SV that had crashed in the 1956 Mille Miglia, and was dubbed 'SVZ'. It had an even lighter body, with rounded lines attributed to Ercole Spada, and it was reckoned that even with a normal engine the aerodynamic improvements yielded as much as a 10mph (16kph) gain on top speed. Success in racing led to a demand for replicas and a handful were built in 1957-59, with minor body variations and usually with engines tuned by independents, notably Conrero.

The 'official' SZ was first shown at Geneva in 1960. The basic short-wheelbase Spider platform was used for the production cars, unlike Zagato's early cars which had the longer Sprint chassis, with engines in states of tune to give at least 112bhp. That was the catalogue figure, but of course any Italian contender with serious intentions

would have had his engine prepared in one of the specialist boutiques. Late cars had outputs approaching 125bhp, while development engines gave some 130bhp. The five-speed gearbox from the SS was used.

A tubular frame carried thin aluminium body panels, usually unprotected by front or rear bumpers. The lines were stubby and rounded, in sharp contrast to the sleek SS, with aerodynamics which were obviously just as effective. The fascia layout and steering wheel were familiar from the SS, while the rest of the interior, with its competition seats, general lack of trim and sliding plastic side windows (the wind-up windows seen on some early cars were more susceptible to scratch marks), emphasised the car's sporting purpose. In a late modification the rear of the bonnet was curved up to allow air to exit to the windscreen. Apart from an Alfa badge on the nose and a 'Z' above the indicator repeaters behind the front wheels, the car was not usually badged.

Zagato's original cars were some 110kg (242lb) lighter than the Sprint Veloce, while the 'official' cars were about 82kg (180lb) lighter. The lower weight was said to benefit road-holding and handling, while in measurable performance it made for improvements in acceleration but not in top gear speed, at least with the normal top gear ratio that it shared with the SS. Higher speed gains

The way the tail of the SS falls away sharply gives minimal boot space, especially as the compartment is occupied by the spare wheel and the battery. The badges were the principal distinguishing detail, the Giulia's being much less ornate than the Giulietta's.

came after wind-tunnel work by the factory led to a long nose and the fashionable Kamm tail. These featured on the last 44 production cars ('SZT' or 'SZ2'), and to a degree heralded the lines of the next variant, the GTZ.

The specification and lines of the SS, together with the 'thoroughbred' background, tempted amateurs to use the car in races and rallies, where its weight told against

Studio view emphasises Zagato's clean lines for the SZ, seen here without the Plexiglass headlight fairings that were sometimes fitted. This early car has slender side grilles and separate sidelights.

it. Although the car had been launched at Monza, no real effort was put into developing it or into weight reduction, Alfa conceding that it had no competition ambitions for the car. In any case it would have been pitched against the SZ, which really was a successful competition model. To Alfa Romeo that meant successes in racing – rallies were incidental.

In racing there were class victories at Daytona and Sebring, as well as in the Targa Florio and secondary events on the Italian mainland. The original Zagato car had won its class in the 1957 Coppa Intereuropa GT race, and the same event in 1959 saw an Alfa Romeo 1-2-3 in the 1300cc class. In 1961 Elio Zagato, the son of the company founder and a moving force behind the SZ, was second in the class, sandwiched between a pair of Fiat-Abarths. Incidentally, later in the 1960s the Fittipaldi brothers, Emerson and Wilson, raced an SZ in Brazil before they moved to Europe. Photographs suggest that it had a hard life, and it carried prominent sponsor names before Colin Chapman introduced this mixed blessing to the circuits of the Old World.

The tough little coupé was to gain an excellent record on fast tarmac rallies, and in the most demanding rallies on loose surfaces. Victories for Bernard Consten's French-entered SZ in the Alpine Rally and the Liège-Rome-Liège in 1958 were outstanding, and a hat trick of Alfa class wins in the Alpine 1300cc class included a 1-2-3 in 1963, when a Conrero-developed car headed a normal SZ. Crewed by Rolland and Augias, it was the only GT car to complete the event without penalty. The best overall result for an SZ in 1959 was second place in the Sestrières Rally, and then there was another Alpine win in 1960, for de Lageneste in a French SZ.

The record of the SZ encouraged the development of a more specialised competition car that was to incorporate Giulia components and be linked to the production car in its designation. This was the Giulia TZ or *Tubolare Zagato*, soon to be referred to as the GTZ or more popularly as the *Tubolare*. Alfa set up a competitions subsidiary, playing a role not dissimilar to that of the defunct Alfa Corse, to handle the programme. In-house design work started in 1959. The project was headed by Giuseppe Busso, a designer and development engineer who served with Fiat in the 1930s, became involved with the outstanding Alfa Romeo 158 Grand Prix car, and then spent time with Ferrari before rejoining Alfa. Senior members of the design group were Edo Mazoni, responsible for the space-frame, and Livio Nicolis of the experimental department, while Satta exercised overall control of the project.

Work on production cars took priority in Satta's department, so when GTZ prototype test running started in 1961 it seemed almost incidental, dragging on through 1962 with the aim of the car being raceworthy in 1963. Early in 1962 there were reports of an open two-seater with a 1.6-litre engine developing over 120bhp; during tests at Monza it apparently lapped 5sec faster than a Giulietta SV. Finally, late in 1963, the GTZ made its competition debut…

The Giulia engine, five-speed transmission and front suspension were used in the GTZ, but coil spring and wishbone independent rear suspension took the place of the beam axle. There were Dunlop disc brakes all round, inboard at the rear, and ZF steering. The fuel tank capacity was 100 litres (22.0 Imperial gallons, 26.4 US gallons) compared with the Giulia's 46 litres (10.1 Imperial gallons, 12.2 US gallons); both had a reserve of 7 litres (1.5 Imperial gallons, 1.8 US gallons). The space frame weighed 40kg (88lb), optimum tube thicknesses in that pre-computer age being determined by loading trials. The complex and rigid structure was built by SAI Ambrosini, and Zagato was responsible for the aluminium body. The fuel tank and spare wheel above it

Forerunner of the Giulietta SZ was the Zagato Special. This car at Pau in 1958 has an Abarth to the right. In the smaller GT racing classes the two marques were rivals, and their cars often looked strikingly similar.

filled the tail, while external badging was the same style as used on the SZ.

Interior space was limited by the wide transmission tunnel and low roof, so although the seats were very low, life must have been difficult for tall drivers such as Andrea de Adamich, one of the regulars. In front of the driver there was a large rev counter with tell-tale, flanked by oil and water gauges, while in front of the passenger was an equally large speedometer. Lack of trim testified to the competition intentions, and meant that there was nothing to subdue noise – but then rally crew fatigue would not have figured prominently in the circuit-oriented minds at Alfa Romeo. Quarter lights and small opening panels in the side windows provided some ventilation.

The production SZ was sleeker, and this 'official' 1961 car shows many minor changes, including a more penetrating nose, secondary lights outside the grille, neater headlight treatment, badging in line with other Giulietta models, sensible door handles and revised side windows. From the rear the efficient Kamm tail of later SZs can be seen.

Consten and de Lageneste raising dust with an SZ in the 1958 Liège-Rome-Liège (left), and with silverware overflowing the bonnet of the same car after their victory in the Alpine Rally later that year (below). On the left is the class-winning Giulietta TI driven by Clarou and Gele.

The *Tubolare* was light, officially 650kg (1433lb) but with 10kg (22lb) soon being added. The engine gave 112bhp in the catalogue form and up to 170bhp in the works circuit cars in 1965. Alfa Romeo claimed a top speed of 'more than 200kph' (125mph) for the GTZ – a recurrent figure in the Giulietta and Giulia story!

Construction of the 100 cars called for to meet Group 4 homologation requirements was contracted out to the small Chizzola company's Autosport workshops at Udine. The Alfa Romeo policy calling for a subsidiary to run its works cars and assist private owners, laid down by Chairman Giuseppe Luraghi and commercial director Iginio Aloisio, led to Autodelta being set up under *Ing* Carlo Chiti and *Ing* Ludovico Chizzola. In 1964 the GTZ operation was moved from Udine to Autodelta's new base at Settimo Milanese, just to the west of Milan and conveniently close to the main Alfa plant at Arese.

Chiti personified the Italian automotive engineer of

SZ development car. The tubular members carried the bodywork, rather than performing a **chassis function. Gearbox protrudes well back into the cockpit, where the seat is mounted low.**

Broadside view
emphasises the SZ's crisp
but dumpy lines (top).
The car in the 1990
Eurotrophaeum, a tour of

12 European capitals to
mark Alfa's 80th
anniversary (above)
shows off its larger grille
with integral side lights.

Waiting for 4.00pm one
Saturday at the Le Mans
24 Hours in 1963. The
two Kamm-tailed, rug-
covered, Alfa SZs were

to last for seven hours
(35, driven by Biscaldi
and 'Kim') and 16 hours
(34, driven by Sala and
Rossi).

The *Tubolare* – the TZ – was a purposeful car, and very smooth in its first form, although the mirrors and bonnet straps would have induced unnecessary aerodynamic drag.

the post-war decade, and was to continue in this vein long after his methods had become outmoded. From 1953 he had worked for four years under Nicolis in the Alfa Romeo special engineering department, then had a spell with Ferrari as chief engineer, before two years with the hapless ATS venture. He 'came home' to Alfa, to a glorious period in the 1960s and a sad decline in the late 1970s, and an inept Grand Prix programme that became a millstone. A consequence was that Autodelta lost its semi-independent role, and its operations were wound down. A few years later a new Alfa Corse was to win circuit racing championships for Alfa Romeo.

The Autodelta story opened with a promising *Tubolare* chapter, and it hardly matters that this looks better on paper than it was in reality, for there were few other contenders in the TZ's capacity class through 1964 and 1965. The car's long gestation period followed by changes in objectives meant that it had a relatively short front-line life. The first cars were run by Eugenio Dragoni's Sant'Ambroeus team late in 1963, before Autodelta became the works team.

The TZ2 appeared in 1965 almost as an indulgence, for it would be run for little more than one season, there was no obvious threat to Alfa's class superiority and Autodelta was already developing a Giulia derivative for racing in 1966. A 'G' or Giulia reference was omitted from the designation but the tail was badged 'Giulia TZ', while Autodelta's triangle badge joined the 'Z' on the flanks and the Alfa badge on the nose. Outwardly, there

The purposeful cockpit of a TZ. The rev counter is ahead of the driver, flanked by water and oil pressure gauges, and oddly with the important oil temperature gauge low on the left. The large speedometer is in the centre of the fascia.

The GTZ, *Tubolare*, was a highly specialised Giulia variant, with a recessed – and individualistic – tail treatment. The tubular chassis (below), showing the independent rear suspension and inboard rear disc brakes ahead of the large fuel tank.

were wider wheels, additional intakes above the stylised Alfa grille of the TZ2, and a lowered roofline that sloped less towards the tail, which was more sharply cut off with a larger recessed flat area. The arrangement of the fuel tanks (with quick filler on the right) and the spare wheel mounting followed the TZ. The cockpit reflected experience, with some rearrangement of the instruments; they were hooded, and the large speedo in front of the passenger was sunk into the fascia. Two dozen of these second-generation cars were built, half of them with glass-fibre bodies made by Balzarotti. The cars tended to vary in detail, such as the occasional use of small air scoops behind the side windows, and in the engines, which included a dry sump variation.

Alfa Romeo had a very successful season in 1964, with many class victories, most of them gained with Giulia TI saloons. However, class wins in major events fell to TZs, at Sebring, in the Targa Florio (third and fourth overall were notable results), at the Nürburgring (11th and 12th overall) at Le Mans (13th and 15th overall), in the Tour de France and in the Tour de Corse. Jean Rolland won his second *Coupe* for a penalty-free run in the 1964 Alpine Rally, and two years later won his third, also driving an Alfa Romeo, to become one of the select quartet to win a silver *Coupe*. Further down the scale there were class wins in the Intereuropa Cup at Monza and in the Paris 1000Km, and, importantly from a marketing point of view, the Watkins Glen Road Racing Championship class fell to a TZ. In 1965 there were class

The shadows are long at Alfa's Balocco test track as Andrea de Adamich (black helmet) makes a point to fellow *Tubolare* drivers Teodoro Zeccoli and Ignazio Giunti (light helmet). Carlo Chiti, the Autodelta boss, is to Zeccoli's left.

The *Tubolare*'s European career wound down in 1966, and this car was campaigned in Australia in 1967 by an Alfa-loyal team. It is flanked at Warwick Farm by a GTA and the Alfa-engined Mildren-Waggott Tasman single-seater.

Pit stop for the *Tubolare* driven by Businello and Deserti into 13th place at Le Mans in 1964.

developed a twin-plug cylinder head. This was not an innovation, but Chiti deserves credit for its application. As far as Autodelta was concerned, the twin-spark heads were to be more important in the GTA, its main car in 1966. There was an intriguing yardstick in the 1965 Nürburgring 1000Km race: Autodelta ran a GTA coupé in the prototype category and it finished just two places behind the best-placed, class-winning TZ that was shared by two rather more prominent drivers…

The *Tubolare* hardly featured in European Rally Championship events in 1965, although there was a lowly 13th on the Alpine, but a Swiss pair placed one second in the GT category of the Marathon de la Route and there were class successes in secondary events such as the Geneva Rally. In retrospect it is a little surprising that the TZ was not more prominent in the then-important European Hill Climb Championship – in 1965 it gained just one top six placing in the seven events.

Racing attention switched to Group 2 touring cars in 1966 but the TZ2s were still active, run by Autodelta through to the early-summer Nürburgring 1000Km race, in which Bianchi and Schultze placed one 13th overall and won the Production Sports 1600cc class. Afterwards the cars were sold to private owners. Earlier in the year there had been class wins in the Sebring 12 Hours and the Monza 1000Km. Although they drove an Alfa into fourth place in the wet Targa Florio, Pinto and Todaro were only third in their class, behind the Porsches placed first and third overall.

wins for TZs at Sebring, in Sicily and at the Nürburgring, although the four cars which started at Le Mans all retired, one when 11th overall. The TZ2 made its major race debut in the Targa Florio, running as high as ninth before retiring.

To wring out the 170bhp claimed for these cars, the compression ratio was increased to 11.4:1 and Autodelta

Road variants ....

Coachbuilders also created road cars in this little series of Giulietta and Giulia derivatives. In 1964 Bertone showed the Giulia-based *Canguro* coupé, echoing its earlier *Tubolare* body styling exercise with a softer version of the TZ. Giugiaro gave *Canguro* more rounded lines than the TZs, with a deeper nose and a lower frontal area. Windscreen and door glass curved into the roof, which could well have made for production problems if the project had got that far (although it made entry and exit easy for tall drivers), and combined with the large rear window it promised a considerable greenhouse effect. But at least through-flow ventilation was provided, with air exhausting through the *quadrifoglio* behind each door, and the glass-fibre seats were covered with loose-weave breathing fabric. The seats played a part in keeping the height down to 41.7in (106cm), for they were sunk into the floorplan to the extent that they determined ground clearance. The 13in Campagnolo wheels also helped to make the car low.

Canguro appeared fully furnished on the Bertone show stands at Paris and Turin, and although it was presented as a styling exercise it seemed to be a practical proposition, engineered for production with a body that could be replicated in plastics. It was developed with Alfa Romeo technical collaboration, and Bertone handed it over to Alfa at the end of 1964. A modest production run could have capitalised on the *Tubolare* image, but Alfa Romeo was experiencing a sales downturn and efforts were concentrated on main-line models.

Pininfarina 'closed the loop' with a rebodied and civilised *Tubolare* exhibited at the 1965 Turin Motor Show. This had an extended nose that looked very

This 1965 TZ2, recognised by its altered window treatment and extra cooling apertures at the front, has Autodelta's triangular badge on the nose and side (above). The smooth, rounded lines of Bertone's *Canguro* (below) are in sharp contrast to the aggressive TZ2.

vulnerable, with a squashed version of the Alfa shield grille flanked by thin horizontal slots which echoed the Spider theme, being swept round almost to the wheel arches. Headlights were faired into the wings, which rose well above the bonnet, and the Kamm tail gave way to a long, slender rear-end treatment. The interior was fully equipped, with two reclining seats, carpeting, heater and proper ventilation. This very pretty little car complemented the purposeful racing coupés admirably, but like *Canguro* it was a one-off.

THE GIULIA

Classic coupés clearly have a shared bloodline in profile view: the Giulietta (left) and the Giulia (below). Neither has much embellishment, nor did they need it. The Giulietta has Alfa badges on its wheel trims, whereas the Giulia wheels simply have the name spelled out. The later car displays the *quadrifoglio* on its rear pillar.

A 'new Giulietta' had been anticipated in speculative reports in the early 1960s, before the Giulia was announced in June 1962 in saloon, coupé and spider forms. At that time only the saloon design was really new, for the Giulietta coupé and spider bodies were carried over with minimal changes. But they had the new name and, more to the point, the 1570cc Giulia engine and the five-speed gearbox.

The boxy lines of the saloon obviously owed much to engineers and little to stylists. They stemmed from the front-wheel drive *Tipo* 103, which followed the Mini layout but did not progress beyond the prototype stage. However, the advantages of the *Tipo* 103 packaging of engine, passenger and boot space were not lost on Satta when the front-engined, rear-drive Giulia was laid out, for the car provided ample room for five people and their luggage within a wheelbase of 98.5in (250cm) and an overall length of 163in (414cm). Outwardly, it was a distinctive car, and its appearance belied its aerodynamic efficiency. This was complemented by the 1570cc engine which was within an Italian 1600cc tax band and fitted into a sports capacity category. A Giulia TI Super was to come in 1963, with its engine in the slightly more powerful form shared with the sporting versions, and there would be a 1300 TI in 1966.

The Giulia saloons formed the backbone of the Alfa Romeo ranges until 1972, with sales exceeding 456,000 – well over double the number of coupés and Spiders sold in the same period.

The engine, already mentioned as the Giulietta 1600 SS power unit, naturally had the same make-up as the first 'small' derivatives of the 1900 straight four. Both bore and stroke were enlarged, from the 74mm × 75mm of the 1290cc engine to 78mm × 82mm, and the quoted power rating increase was in the order of 12bhp, to 92bhp at 6200rpm. The Giulia Sprint and Spider, and the TI Super, had two twin-choke Weber carburettors at first, then two Solex 32 PA1A, with the second choke brought into operation in response to induction airflow at wide throttle openings. There was also a change to Bosch electrics.

Interim coupés and spiders ....

This 1570cc engine was used in the existing coupé and spider bodies, which became the Giulia Sprint and Giulia Spider. The latter was distinguished from its Giulietta predecessor by a shallow intake across the top of the bonnet, aligned with the back of the radiator. This was a much prettier stylist's way to accommodate the greater bonnet height called for by the slightly taller engine than the 'power bulge' to which manufacturers north of the English Channel resorted when coping with similar problems. Otherwise, chrome '1600' figures on the flanks and tails of the two models were the only outward identification.

The five-speed gearbox (with top gear an overdrive) was fitted, with a floor gearchange taken for granted. Three leading shoe drum brakes at the front were inherited from the Giulietta SS/SZ, and there were two leading shoe drums at the rear with, later, Dunlop discs on all four wheels. Despite the assumed superiority of rack and pinion steering, recirculating ball or worm and roller systems were specified, and these proved to be quite satisfactory.

Cockpits were changed little, but seats and some sectors of visibility came in for criticism (not, of course, with the hood-down open car). Controls were precise

The internal test facility at Arese in the late 1960s, with most of the company's models in shot – a GTA in the foreground, and Giulia coupés, spiders and saloons scattered around.

but the instruments, although adequate, were not all easy to read and the glass picked up some reflections.

These intermediate coupés and spiders were well received, for their performance was competitive, and in the first half of the 1960s testers did not regard components like drum brakes as dated, which they might have done later in the decade. *The Autocar* tested a Sprint, while *Road & Track* assessed two Spiders, almost two years apart and in different specifications; the TI figures provide useful comparison.

	Max speed	0-60 mph	Standing ¼-mile
The Autocar (Sprint)	108mph/174kph	13.2sec	18.8sec
Road & Track (Spider)	107mph/172kph	12.2sec	19.0sec
Road & Track (Spider Veloce)	109mph/175kph	10.5sec	17.4sec
The Motor (TI saloon)	103.4mph/166.4kph	13.4sec	19.0sec

The Autocar found this Giulia Sprint as stimulating as the Giulietta: 'Though the appeal of such a car must lie primarily in its performance, the Giulia's has not been achieved by cheese-paring on interior trim or appointments or by a general cutting down of weight.' The report concluded: 'The Giulia Sprint is an interesting mixture of the very good – and the ordinary. It is refined and well-found; moreover, it is tractable and docile, pulling away almost like a 'steamer' from 12mph on fifth gear. Thanks in part to the good body shape the car offers real fuel economy at high speeds.' In fact, overall, the test recorded 26.7mpg (10.6 litres per 100km). *Road & Track* commented that the Spider proved, 'once again that a well-developed old design is always better than an under-developed new design', and pointed out that 'it is one of the least expensive sports car available today with an overhead camshaft engine' – it might have written twin-cam, in which case it really was a bargain.

The American magazine's report on the Spider Veloce concluded: 'All things considered, the Alfa Romeo 1600 Veloce is an excellent sports car by any standards; its responsiveness, accurate handling and ease of operation make it a continuing pleasure for either the skilled driver or the novice, and it undoubtedly has all those intangible personality factors which have always enabled Alfas to form close, rewarding relationships with their owners'. Clearly such cars are not just inanimate objects.

The Spider Veloce, with the high-compression

The boot space in the Giulia Spider was unchanged (below), and more generous than the coupé's, in this case an early GTV.

engine rated at 112bhp, had a claimed top speed of 112mph (180kph), a little more than *Road & Track*'s testers achieved. It also had disc brakes, making it the most desirable of the first spider line. It arrived in 1964 and just over 1000 were built before it was discontinued the following year. There was not a corresponding 101-series Giulia Sprint Veloce.

In 1965 *Road & Track* also published a 30,000-mile (48,000km) report on a Giulia Sprint. The overall cost per mile was 9.68 cents and $442.76 had been spent on repairs and replacements, including a $302.32 bill for a gearbox rebuild and brake relining at 24,000 miles. The quality of both interior and exterior trim was criticised, but the car was bought for pleasure and the owner concluded that his investment had been exceptionally productive. The cost-per-mile figure took account of the car's value at the end of the period, and it was close to the figure for a V8 Mercury Marauder! In depreciation, the Giulia Sprint did not show too well in a contemporary National Automobile Dealers Used Car Guide listing for sports cars, only the MGB having a worse percentage loss figure.

The Giulia Sprint stayed in production until 1964. Meanwhile, the Sprint GT had been seen at a factory preview before its public debut at the 1963 Frankfurt Motor Show, and because it overlapped the last of the Giulietta models in showrooms into 1965 some useful 'neutral' Swiss comparisons can be made.

	Price (Swiss Francs)	Max speed (kph/mph)
Alfa Romeo Giulietta Sprint 130013,950		165/102
Giulia Spider	13,950	172/107
Giulia SS	18,900	195/121
Giulia Sprint GT	16,900	180/112
Giulia TZ	29,850	200/125
Alpine A110 coupé	16,800	180/112
Fiat 1600S Pininfarina coupé	17,900	175/109
Glas 1300ST coupé	14,950	170/106
Lotus Elan S2	18,600	205/127
MGB	11,800	160/100
Morgan 4/4 Series V	9,500	150/93
Porsche 356 1600C coupé	18,500	175/109

Giugiaro's coupé . . . .

The Giulia Sprint GT had familiar mechanical elements with a new coupé body that would continue until the second half of the 1970s, on the 2000 GTV. This was the

The Giulietta Spider body was adopted for the Giulia Spider, but an identification point was the transverse bonnet-top 'intake' trim, necessitated by the height of the engine.

body designed by Giorgio Giugiaro in a hotel room at Bra, not far from Bertone's Turin headquarters. The design had been submitted to Alfa Romeo and approved in the summer of 1960. It was to be built by Alfa Romeo in its new plant at Arese, rather than by Bertone.

The lines reflected Giugiaro's 2600 Sprint, his first design for Bertone – indeed early press descriptions reported that the Giulia Sprint GT was a spin-off from that car. Similarities were especially noticeable at the nose, for Giugiaro broke with the tradition of headlights at the front of the wings and placed them within the front grille. In other respects, for example in the flanks, the two cars had distinct differences. The Sprint GT had the usual bold Alfa shield centrepiece to the grille, with the headlights inboard of turn indicators that were neatly incorporated in the front of each wing. The four headlights of later top-of-the-range models did not make for a visual improvement.

The front-hinged bonnet top had a subtle curve, and soon gained a slim transverse inlet on the hinge line.

Running fore and aft above the level of the wheel arches and below the door handles was a pronounced 'tumblehome', a distinct break line that made trim such as a chrome strip unnecessary. The tail fell away slightly behind the rear window to a rounded lip above a flat back panel. The small bumpers, much better suited to

From the rear '1600' badge identifies the Giulia Spider. Dashboard was little changed from the Giulietta Spider, but instrument faces were different, with a more modern design.

small Italian front number plates than those required in more northerly European countries, did not have over-riders. Brightwork decoration was minimal, with small Bertone badges behind the front wheel arches and an Alfa Romeo script on the back of the boot lid.

The existing suspension was carried over, with minor improvements and a reduction in the number of greasing points, soon obviated altogether, save for the front wheel bearings. The 4½J × 15 wheels (but later 4½J × 14) carried Pirelli Cinturato S tyres or sometimes Michelin XA. Dunlop-developed disc brakes were used all round but the drum handbrake that was inset at the rear was not wholly efficient, an Alfa Romeo trait that long resisted the march of progress.

The engine bay was full, but items such as the plugs and the distributor were easily accessible. The double overhead camshaft four had twin Weber 40 DCOE4 carburettors, but initially it was not in the highest state of tune and was rated at 106bhp (later engine swaps could account for variations). When the car was announced the claimed top speed was 112mph (180kph), but Alfa President *Dott* Giuseppe Luraghi suggested that 125mph could be realised. That faithful 200kph again!

Within the balanced exterior lines, Giugiaro contrived to improve on the preceding Sprint's cabin space, despite a slightly shorter wheelbase. But this was

Late-1960s noses varied. The Sprint GT had an eight-bar grille (top left) while the Junior had a single bar: the 1300 (above left) had normal side lights, but the Junior 1.6 (top right) had horizontal combined side lights and turn indicators. Wheel trims also varied. The later GT 1300 Junior of 1974-76 was a 2000 GTV variant, largely for the Italian market (above right).

still not the full four-seater the company had projected, and after a while Alfa began to come clean and refer to the Sprint GT as a 2+2.

In some respects the interior failed to live up to the elegance of the body, with plenty of shiny black vinyl trim and some cheap fittings. The thin-rimmed two-spoke steering wheel at least gave an uninterrupted view of the main instruments, the paired rev counter on the left and speedometer on the right being flanked by secondary instruments. The five-speed gearbox was light and positive to use, its lever having long fore-and-aft throws and short lateral movement from 1-2 to 3-4. The controversial pedal arrangement, with bottom-hinged clutch and brake and pendant accelerator, was retained.

This time there was acceptable boot space, with the spare wheel under the floor and the battery now in the front of the engine compartment.

Cabriolet

Touring converted 1000 Sprint GTs into soft-top GTCs, a tenth of them being completed in right-hand drive form. The strengthening called for was achieved at some cost to passenger space, and, according to a test in *The Autocar*, without giving acceptable rigidity. There were four seats, but width for the rear pair was restricted by the stowage space for the soft-top supports, while leg room was not generous. Four wind-up side windows were provided, and the top folded away neatly. Following an earlier American trend, a steel hard-top was also available.

The performance of the GTC was similar to the Sprint GT and, importantly, *The Autocar* found that, 'it handles impeccably with all the precision and predictable behaviour which have kept Alfa models so well established in sports car markets throughout the world'. This reflected the general praise for the GTC when it was

introduced in 1965, but the market for four-seater convertibles was modest and production ceased in 1966, the year that a new spider, the Duetto, arrived.

The GTV...

A Sprint GT Veloce (GTV), was inevitable, although surprisingly it was not announced until spring 1966. The designation implied a power plant uprating; the increase of only 3bhp, to 109bhp, was small in terms of maximum output, but the torque curve of an already notably flexible engine was improved and the real performance gains came in acceleration.

The front bucket seats of the GTV were a positive advance, for they were much more supportive than the Sprint GT seats. However, the relationship of seat to pedals and steering wheel was still decidedly 'Italian', forcing tall drivers to adopt a splay-leg position. The instruments were unchanged but looked better in a 'wood-effect' fascia, and a three-spoke steering wheel was normal, with horn 'buttons' in the spokes. Deeply dished rear seats gave a little more space for rear passengers.

The first GTV style, with turn indicators in the nose of the wings and with inset headlights and a three-bar grille. This is *Road & Track*'s **test car.**

A modified grille was an identification feature, with three bold horizontal bars backed by black mesh on each side of the stylised centre in place of the nine thin bars of the Sprint GT. There were also discreet clover leaf insignia on the rear pillars and 'Veloce' script on the rear panel.

On the road, the light and positive GTV inspired confidence. As with the earlier cars, there was some engine noise, but it was an alloy unit with overhead camshafts, after all, and the sounds were in character. In 1967 a GTV was tested by *Road & Track*, which found 'all the traditional Alfa virtues and vices: superb handling, gearbox and finish; minimal heating and ventilation'. It also reported a former Chrysler engineer's reaction to its handling, quoting 'how the devil do they do that with a live rear axle?'. Maximum speed matched the 112mph (180kph) claimed, with 0-60mph in 10.5sec and the standing ¼-mile in 17.6sec.

From any aspect, Giugiaro's coupé – this is a Giulia Sprint GT – was a balanced design. Inside, the simple dashboard (bottom) has a grey 'crackle' finish.

Juniors ....

The last Sprint GTs were completed in 1966, although the model was still listed early in 1967, and the GTV continued for another year with the last few being completed just as 1750 production got into its stride. Meanwhile, an 'economy' coupé, the GT 1300 Junior, had been introduced in September 1966 using the 1290cc engine, developing 103bhp at 6000rpm, to propel a fairly light car with a kerb weight that rose from 930kg (2026lb) to 990kg (2183lb) in the course of production. The body was identified by two headlights whereas the larger-engined model had four, and the words 'GT 1300 Junior' on the rear of the boot lid. The interior trim was plainer, and while the earliest cars had instruments similar to the Sprint GT's (with the outer dials still liable to pick up side window reflections), a new arrangement with the two main dials in binnacles ahead of the steering wheel soon became established. With this change, the subsidiary instruments found a place below the centre of the fascia.

Carrozzeria Touring had produced bodies for the larger Alfas, but GTC was its first Giulietta/Giulia body. This open conversion was aesthetically pleasing, although not quite the full four-seater this happy quartet suggests (right).

The GT 1300 Junior sold particularly well in Italy. There was also to be a GT 1600 Junior coupé from 1972 to 1976. Its 1570cc engine was rated at 110bhp until 1974 and gave a claimed maximum speed of 115mph (185kph), but then the slightly less powerful version used in the contemporary Spider was installed.

At the Turin Motor Shows in 1969 and 1972 Zagato introduced the Junior Z, with a sleek fastback body, in 1300 and then 1600 forms. These models had steel bodywork and were only slightly lighter than early-1970s Juniors, so despite appearances they were only a little quicker. The interior was improved, notably in the fascia with its inset main instruments and the secondary dials ranged at the same level to the driver's right, with further minor improvements in the 1600. The pretence of two tiny rear seats was perpetuated and behind them was a luggage platform, offering reasonable space but with the contents fully exposed to view through the large rear glass areas. The luggage platform was also high and therefore not easy to load – good looks usually come at a

The entry-model price of the Juniors was reflected in the interior fittings, with simple seats and no centre console ahead of the gear lever (the secondary dials had top fixings to the fascia). Switches on the left are unmarked, and choke and hand throttle are below the column.

price. The nose treatment was unusual in that it was faced with transparent plastic, except for a shield-shaped hole in the centre.

The first Junior Z cost only 25 per cent more than a normal Junior coupé as Zagato went to some lengths to keep costs down, so it is surprising that these distinctive cars were not more widely seen, but little effort seems to have been made to market them widely outside Italy and Zagato built only 1510.

The Junior Z Sperimentale of 1971 was a very different creation, its similarities not extending far back from the nose, except that the fascia appeared to have been taken from the Junior Z. It promised to be a hot two-seater coupé, with a 1992cc engine mounted transversely behind the cockpit and drawing its air through an intake on the roof. The rear quarters had distinctive black louvres flanking the large rear window and there was a prominent lip above the flat tail.

The GT 1300 Junior was produced until 1974, and late-1960s cars were tested by *Motor* and *Autocar* in the UK, where the model effectively replaced the Sprint GT sold in the UK between 1963-67. Performance figures were similar.

Interior of a well-used early GTV (top), with a nicely-presented set of instruments, the familiar unlabelled switches, the angled gear lever (taking the most direct route to the 'box) and a footwell storage bin. The 2000 (above) has better seats, eyeball vents, a deeply-dished wheel and a cluster of minor dials between the 'big two'.

Both found that the smaller engine revved freely, but that the gearbox had to be used more to maintain brisk progress. *Motor* summed up the GT 1300 Junior as having 'reasonable seating for three or four people…not particularly fast…highly desirable piece of machinery', while *Autocar* found it 'much refined and quieter' with 'good open-road performance from a small engine, lacking bottom-end punch only'.

1750 GTV..

As the first Juniors slipped into a defined market slot, the need for a larger engine at the other end of the range was

	Max speed	0-60mph	Standing ¼-mile
Motor	102mph/164kph	13.8sec	19.6sec
Autocar	102mph/164kph	13.2sec	19.1sec

The 1750 GTV (right) and 2000 GTV (below) compared. The smaller 14in wheels make for a change of stance, and outward differences reflect the effort to move Alfa Nord products up-market in the 1970s. The 2000 GTV has a more elaborate grille, over-riders, indicator repeaters, 'exposed nut' wheels and, unseen here, a more luxurious interior.

identified, and in 1968 a bored and stroked (80mm × 88.5mm) 1779cc unit was introduced. Rather than being termed '1800', the three-model range was named after the 1930s Alfa classic – the 1750 – also recalled in the Zagato 4R (see page 51). The enlarged engine had a stiffer block, and an alternator was used in place of a dynamo. In 1968 no cars were exported to the USA, because there was a delay while the Alfa-Spica fuel injection was finalised. This system was to replace the Webers on US cars in order to meet emissions requirements and maintain power output. When the Spica system later became notorious for its unreliability, the Alfa part of the name was diplomatically dropped…

This coupé retained the familiar Bertone body, with fatter wheels and turn indicators between bumper and outer main lights. There was better sound damping and the cabin was improved, with another change in seats when the front passenger was provided with a head rest, as a dozing support rather than for safety reasons. The speedometer and rev counter were well positioned in hooded surrounds which projected slightly above the fascia, while the secondary instruments were on the centre console. There was a three-spoke wood-rim steering wheel.

The suspension was changed in detail, with anti-roll bars at front and rear, but generally the characteristics of

the car were unchanged, even down to the tendency to lift an inside wheel in fast cornering. A twin-circuit braking system came in 1969.

The Berlina saloon, coupé (GT Veloce) and two-seater (Spider Veloce) all had the same 132bhp engine and unusually *Motor* tested all three within a year, with these results:

	Kerb weight	Max speed	0–60 mph
Berlina	2363lb/1072kg	110mph/177kph	10.2sec
GTV	2240lb/1016kg	115.5mph/185.5kph	9.3sec
Spider	2229lb/1011kg	116.4mph/187kph	9.2sec

The speeds presumably reflected weight as well as aerodynamics, and overall fuel consumption ranged from 23.4mpg (12.1 litres per 100km) in the GTV to 24.1mpg (11.7 litres per 100km) in the Spider.

A *Road & Track* long-term assessment of the 1750 GTV produced a cost-per-mile figure of 11.5 cents. *Autocar* staff were enthusiastic about their long-term GTV, in which a sensitive driver 'rediscovers the pure pleasure of motoring'. Its costs for 10,000 miles, excluding fuel, were £968.18. Finally, *Road & Track* included a 1750 GTV in its Best Ten Cars listing in 1971,

as the Best Sports/GT Car in the $4500–$6500 category: 'As with other fine automobiles, the keyword for the Alfa Romeo 1750 is balance. Everything is blended together masterfully...'

2000 GTV

Such praise was fine, but Alfa Romeo had already accepted that a still larger engine was called for, because 1750 sales had never come up to expectations, and were falling as the 1970s opened. The step up had been too

The Junior Z was elegantly styled by Zagato, with the curiosity of Perspex enclosing most of the nose. Its cockpit layout (facing page) was perhaps the best of any of the Giulia models to that time and the main Jaeger instruments are admirably clear, but provision for luggage was sacrificed to body styling. On this model the Alfa shield did not contain an emblem.

timid, so in 1971 there was another engine stretch, to 1962cc (84mm × 88.5mm). Power outputs were to vary fractionally over the years: at the outset the stated ratings were 132bhp on Weber carburettors or 127bhp in fuel-injected US form, but the figures soon became 131bhp and 129bhp respectively. The revised coupé model became the 2000 GTV, and a 2-litre coupé designated 1750 GTAm that had been doing well on the circuits in 1970 became the 2000 GTAm, without a change in its engine capacity…

The 2000 GTV had a limited-slip differential to help put the power on the road, but there were few other changes because the saloon and coupé were increasingly stopgaps as new cars were developed, and the company entered another difficult period. The coupé body was still handsome, although its high waist line was beginning to make it look rather dated. The 2000 GTV had another revised multi-bar grille, and reversing lights were incorporated in the rear lights cluster.

The main instruments now flanked the small fuel and water temperature gauges and warning lights, as the centre console was modified. At the same time the air vents were made more efficient, and air conditioning was to become a late option, hence the console changes. Oddly, after years insisting that the coupés were four-

seaters, then that they had 2+2 accommodation, Alfa Romeo proclaimed them two-seaters in the USA, apparently because it was not possible to meet a Federal requirement for rear seat safety belts – but the little rear seats were still there.

Testers failed to reach the 195kph/121mph claimed for the 2000 GTV:

	Max speed	0-60 mph	Standing ¼-mile
Motor	115.3mph/185.7kph	8.9sec	16.6sec
Road & Track	110mph/177kph	9.6sec	17.6sec

These figures reflect European and US power outputs, and comments were kind. *Motor*: 'The Alfa bears its years remarkably well…has style and quality'. *Road & Track*: 'The GTV is a good 1964 design, overdue for a change… still a good car and a capable performer… directly competing 2+2 GTs are not formidable enough to embarrass it.'

In this last phase of the coupé's life, these Alfas were not quite so competitively priced in that 'neutral' Swiss market. Some of the cars listed are 'sports' rather than 'GT' but the appeal was similar; representative 1973 prices and claimed top speeds of a dozen cars were:

Harold Radford's attempt to improve the Sprint GT. The Cibié headlights flank a grille in anodised aluminium, additional external trim included 'gravel' rails, and those protruding wire wheels might have been questioned by some traffic authorities. Inside, doors were walnut-capped and the reworked fascia included rosewood facing; there were optional electric windows and air conditioning, pile carpeting and a rear seat Radford termed a 'Cleopatra couch' (the ends of the back were curved, but the actual seat was a narrow bench!).

'Special equipment' versions sometimes helped move cars from dealer forecourts. Among the adornments on this UK-created '2000 GT Veloce SE' is a vinyl roof – a passing fad.

	Price (Swiss francs)	Max speed (kph/mph)
Alfa Romeo GT 1300 Junior	15,600	170/106
GT 1600 Junior	17,100	185/115
2000 GTV	19,700	190/118
Audi 100 Coupé S	20,590	183/114
Datsun 240Z	21,000	205/127
Fiat 124S coupé (1800)	14,450	185/115
Lancia Fulvia HF 1.6	20,750	190/118
Lotus Europa TC	21,500	188/117
MGB GT	15,500	173/107
Porsche 911T coupé	33,700	205/127
Triumph TR6 hard-top	17,650	187/116
Volvo 1800ES	27,800	180/112

In the late 1960s and into the 1970s the GTAs were Alfa's main competition cars, and the 1750s seen on circuits were usually in Group 1 production saloon events, with little or no factory input. This applied even to the race-prepared 1750 GTVs run in the small-car category of the SCCA TransAm series in 1971, while

The first Scarabeo concept car, built in Turin by Osi with Alfa assistance and powered by a rear-mounted Giulia engine.

The Montreal (top) used some GTV equipment, but its engine was a 2.6-litre quad-cam V8. The 'replicar' and the real thing – Zagato's 4R and a 6C-1750 (above). By no stretch of the imagination could one be mistaken for the other...

there was modest support for amateur entrants in the USA. In Britain Roger Clark ran a 2000 GTV pair in 1972, and GTVs were seen in amateur hands elsewhere in Europe and in production classes in rallies.

While the Spider was to continue into the 1990s, the Bertone coupé line ended with the 2000 GTV in 1976, and exports to some markets such as the UK had ended in 1975. It had reached maturity at the beginning of the decade and was perhaps past its prime by mid-decade, when it no longer stood out in a crowd and was seriously dated in some respects, such as boot space. But it had served the company, *Alfisti* and other keen motorists well, with more than 210,000 built.

Variants...

As well as concept cars and the Junior Z, the second half of the 1960s saw two Giulia-based cars at opposite ends of the motoring spectrum – the Zagato 4R of 1965 and the Montreal that appeared as a show car in 1967 and reached production in 1970.

The 4R was sponsored by the magazine *Quattroruote* (meaning four wheels, hence 4R) and was an evocation of the classic Alfa Romeo 6C-1750, which had usually carried Zagato bodies in the early 1930s. But the general reception for this car was not enthusiastic, for the age of the 'replica' was just dawning and there was a mistaken tendency to regard the 4R as a 'counterfeit', although a glance at its wheels and tyres (let alone under its bonnet) would have shown that this could never have been Zagoto's intention.

It was an eye-catching fun car, with performance that was inferior to the Giulia saloon from which it inherited its chassis, engine, transmission and running gear. Zagato added a tubular frame to carry its two-seater body, which sat low and had a very open cockpit. Sidescreens and soft top were provided, but they were tiresome to erect. The wheelbase was extended by an inch, and the track was a little narrower than the Giulia's. The car was some 240kg (528lb) lighter, but its aerodynamic inadequacies meant that the claimed top speed of 97mph (155kph) fell short of the Giulia saloon's 102mph (165kph). The 1930s car which inspired it could reach 106mph (170kph), with a supercharged 1754cc straight-six engine.

The 4R provided Morgan-style motoring at twice the cost of a new Morgan, but it did give its occupants a better ride than the British evergreen. Zagato sold 92 4Rs, and Achilli Motor built a few more with glass-fibre bodies in the mid-1970s under the name Leontina.

The Montreal was built as a show car for Expo '67, an exhibition in Montreal at which Alfa Romeo represented Italy with 'a car showing man's aspirations in the automotive field'. Bertone styled the body on the

The 2000 GTV was a handsome car, although in some respects such as cockpit width it had been overtaken by more modern designs. Driver's view (far left) shows off well-presented instruments, and the 'clap-hands' wipers still used at a late stage. Rear pillar decoration (left) shows Alfa serpent.

floorpan and running gear of a 1750 GTV, and the Expo car had that model's engine. This was replaced by a detuned 2.6-litre version of the quad-cam V8 from the T33 sports racing programme in the production Montreal, which was announced at the 1970 Geneva Motor Show. Intended to be a practical GT car rather than an out-and-out supercar, this was nominally a 2+2 but it was really a two-seater with a miniscule boot.

It looked good, but there were compromises in its make-up. The engine needed cosseting, fuel consumption was frightening, the driving position was poor and the steering heavy. Little thought seemed to have been given to ergonomic aspects and the construction of the steel-bodied production cars included some particularly bad rust traps. Internal problems at Alfa Romeo that led to cost-cutting meant that the Montreal was simply neglected through development and production did not really get under way in 1971. When it trickled to an end

The 2000 GTV remained in production until 1976, but its lines remained as fresh as when Giorgio Giugiaro created them 15 years earlier.

with just 27 cars built in 1977, the total was well short of the 10,000 originally projected. Only 3925 cars were built, just 168 of them in right-hand drive form.

There was Alfa Romeo involvement, and Giulia components such as the engine, in the extraordinary 1966 Scarabeo built by Osi, a little-known Turin coachbuilder which already had a pretty mid-1960s Fiat spider to its credit when this concept car was created under the eye of Alfa engineering chief Busso. The chassis of large-diameter tubes carried the fuel, while the engine was transversely mounted, and offset, behind the cockpit, which had a one-piece cover hinged at the front – an impractical styling fad that went the rounds.

This Scarabeo was followed by two more, one open, the other a coupé, with the engine ahead of the rear axle. Both were low and sleek, and the open car was even reported to have competition potential, but then Italian journalists are ever-hopeful about such things. Neither appeared in public, at a show or on a circuit.

The GTV was not a notable rally car, but was an out of the ordinary choice for amateur entrants. The crew of this 1750 GTV appear to be very relaxed on the 1970 Monte Carlo Rally.

TOURING CAR TRIUMPHS

A new era in saloon car racing opened at Monza in March 1966. Alfa Romeos dominated the first round of the European Touring Car (ETC) Championship with nine GTAs squabbling for the lead during the opening phase, and pulling away from reigning champion Sir John Whitmore in a Lotus Cortina at the rate of seconds a lap. Some of the GTAs faded, but de Adamich/Zeccoli and 'Geki'/Pinto survived the close battles and chaotic pit stops to win convincingly in a pair of Autodelta cars. This was not the first race for the Alfa Romeo GTA, but the result was a true pointer to the successes that would be achieved in the coming seasons of mainstream racing for modified saloons.

The GTA was a competition version of the Sprint GT, which it resembled in appearance. It was a catalogued model and almost 500 examples of the first GTA were to be built in the years 1965-69, followed by a similar number of GTA 1300 Juniors from 1968. There was a standard specification which gives a reference point

Alfas at Monza, and convincing winners too. Pinto heading de Adamich, the eventual winner, in a sister GTA on their way to a team 1-2 in the opening European Touring Car Championship race of the 1966 season.

for the GTA, but apart from departures from standard for circuit or rally use, the GTA *corsa* was more potent, and a cynic might also bear in mind that the first scrutineering haggles came at that early 1966 Monza meeting...

The 'A' indicated *Alleggerita* (lightened). The interior was bare, light alloy panels replaced steel panels, and weight was substantially reduced from the GT Sprint's 965kg (2128lb) to an official 745kg (1640lb) for the 1965 GTA or 820kg (1808lb) for the 1969 version. An addition to the cockpit was an unobtrusive roll bar, and there was of course a competition seat – or seats in the rally cars. The GTA sat on 7in alloy wheels (14in diameter rather than the 15in of the regular coupés) so

A GTA in road trim, not that the circuit car looked very different – it had a competition exhaust and superfluous items such as bumpers were removed. The cockpit was fully equipped with a drilled- spoke wood-rim steering wheel to complement the behaviour and sound of a GTA. Italian advert boasted about one of many European Touring Car successes.

that the fatter tyres fitted within the wheel arches, and the lowered competition suspension incorporated rear axle Panhard rod location and a rear anti-roll bar.

The standard power output of the 1570cc engine was 115bhp, but a lot more was available. The quoted net power was developed at 6000rpm, but Autodelta could produce another 50bhp for clients, and perhaps 170bhp for the team cars, at 7500rpm. The common starting point was a new cylinder head with twin plugs per cylinder (to speed up and spread ignition in the large combustion chamber) and a 9.7:1 compression ratio, while for its own cars Autodelta used up to 10.5:1. Modified starters and dynamos were fitted and there was an oil cooler and a special exhaust exiting under the driver's door, except on cars used on the road or in rallies. The transmission included a heavy-duty clutch, close ratio gears and a special final drive. Normally a 46-litre (10.1 Imperial gallons, 12.1 US gallons) fuel tank was fitted to the GTA, but a 'long-range' 90-litre (19.8 Imperial gallons, 23.8 US gallons) tank was available.

The GTA really looked the part. The cars were usually run without bumpers, and there were simple mesh 'grilles' and a skeletal Alfa shield, with two headlights or a battery of main lights on a rally car. The oil cooler could be seen under the nose, sometimes an old-fashioned bonnet strap was used on a circuit car, small conventional door handles took the place of the occasionally uncooperative recessed finger-tip handles of the normal road models, and the wheels were unadorned. A clover leaf in a white triangle normally appeared behind the front wheels and on the rear panel. Little chrome plates below this emblem on the flanks recorded *disegno di Bertone*, while 'Giulia Sprint GTA' appeared on the end of the boot lid.

These Alfas had the legs of anything else in the category on the circuits in 1966, through corners or on straights. Their promise had been demonstrated in 1965, before they were homologated, notably in the

The GTA 1300 Junior looked purposeful. This road car carries a full complement of badges, including the Autodelta triangle and a bonnet-top serpent. An amazingly clean engine bay shows off the twin-plug version of Alfa's twin-cam engine, which gave up to 170bhp.

Nürburgring 1000Km and in the Spa 24 Hours, when they were second and third.

The 1966 season opened with a dominant assault on the Sebring 4 Hours, Jochen Rindt winning in an Autodelta GTA with other GTAs placed 3-4-5. In Europe there was that early-season Monza victory, and although Ford battled back in the Lotus Cortina's last major season, the GTAs beat them at Zandvoort and then consistently through the rest of the year. Outstanding results included victory over the BMWs in the Nürburgring 6 Hours and on Ford's home territory in the British round of the championship at Snetterton, both races being won by de Adamich and Zeccoli. Alfa Romeo also beat Ford and BMW in the TransAm Championship in the USA.

Alfa Romeo claimed 'more than 200' race victories in 1966, most taken by the GTAs, and some actually class victories. Both the company and Autodelta still tended to stay away from rallies, apart from limited support for competitors in the Italian national series, and although

Jean Rolland's car in the Alpine Rally was to full Autodelta specification it was very much an independent entry, rewarded with outright victory.

In 1967 the Porsche 911 was homologated as a Group 2 car, but even these 2-litre machines were sometimes beaten by the Alfa Romeos, which in any case piled up enough class wins to take the European title again. Britain's oldest established motor race, the Tourist Trophy, fell to Andrea de Adamich in a GTA in 1967, the year the RAC restored the event to touring car status after two years of questionable sports racing car races. Very much on Porsche territory, the touring car class of

A GTA 1300 Junior performs on a water-drenched skid pan (left). This GTA in 'as-raced' condition (below left) has a place of honour in the Alfa Romeo Museum.

the European Mountain Championship fell to GTA driver Ignazio Giunti. There was also some success for the Group 6 GTA SA in lesser sports car events at various circuits in Europe.

The Geneva Motor Show in 1967 had seen the announcement of the GTA SA, built by Autodelta to Group 6 sports-prototype regulations. This looked like a GTA rather than a traditional sports car, but it had a supercharged 1570cc engine giving 200bhp at 7500rpm. This was a short-stroke unit (86mm × 67.5mm) intended to rev more freely, as two Alfa-designed but Autodelta-made centrifugal superchargers were used. Maximum

power was soon to be matched by a normally-aspirated 2-litre version of the four-cylinder engine. As the ten cars built were to customer order, mainly for German and French clients, the GTA SA was not a diversion from Autodelta's Tipo 33 sports racing programme that was taking shape in 1967. It was modestly successful, winning first time out, at Hockenheim, and proving successful in other secondary races in 1967-68 and also in hillclimbs, to which the characteristics of the engine were probably best suited.

In 1968 the GTA was joined by the GTA 1300 Junior, soon to be known popularly as the GTAJ in Italy. Its body, transmission, suspension and ancillaries were similar, but it had a 1290cc engine. This was not the near-square unit used in the contemporary GT 1300 Junior, having a shorter stroke and increased bore (78mm × 67.5mm), and a twin-plug head. In 1968 it was rated at 96bhp at 6000rpm in 'normal' form, but it was developed to give 160bhp at 7800rpm in racing trim, and a fuel injection version giving 165bhp came later.

The competition objective of the GTA 1300 Junior, of course, was to compete in the capacity division below the GTA, as the winners in each of the three championship classes, or divisions, had equal status. This ploy was completely successful, with Alfa Romeo winning the 1300cc and 1600cc classes in the European

57

Touring Car Championship, while GTA driver Spartaco Dini took the drivers' title in the larger category. Class C in the SCCA series also fell to GTAs. And in 1968 Autodelta ventured into the rally world, successfully in the European series, although from 1970 the name Alfa Romeo did not appear in the points listings apart from an eighth place in the 1972 Alpine.

The last significant GTA victories were scored in 1969 by Spartaco Dini, sharing with 'Riccardone' at Monza and de Adamich at the Nürburgring.

The GTAm arrived to complement the 1.3-litre cars in 1970, the only year that Alfa Romeo had an outright touring car champion, Toine Hezemans – in preceding years this title had been shared with winners of other divisions. The 'm' added to the designation stood for *maggiorate*, which referred to the engine although the bulging wheel arches meant that it could have applied to the appearance of this spectacular car. Alfa's wish to emphasise the link with the normal road 1750 GTV for publicity purposes meant that the car was known as the 1750 GTAm, although the actual engine capacity was 1985cc. Spica fuel injection took the place of the twin Webers of the GTA, the valves were enlarged, bore and stroke were increased to 84.5mm × 88.5m, and the compression ratio was raised to 11.1:1. In its second year this engine gave as much as 220bhp, compared with the 118bhp of the normal 1750 GTV. The coupé lines were retained but the front track was increased, as was weight. In 1971 the GTAm had a claimed top speed not far short of 150mph, and when it became the 215bhp 2000 GTAm in 1973, the top speed of the car was given as 230kph (143mph).

The early 1966 success of the GTA was repeated when Hezemans won the opening ETC race of 1970 at Monza in a GTAm. That was the first of the Dutch driver's four wins in the 1970 series, the others coming at Budapest, Brno and Jarama, and with second placings at the beautiful Salzburgring and the less scenic Silverstone he piled up 48 points in Division III. The Silverstone TT result was particularly significant because Alfa's more powerful rivals, BMW and Chevrolet, might have been expected to have a decisive advantage on this fast circuit. Gianluigi Picchi also scored well, and Nanni Galli co-drove with Hezemans in long races. In Division II Carlo Trucchi only won twice, but scored 38 points with a GTA to take that class and give Alfa Romeo a double. His co-drivers in the two winning races were 'Chico' and Carlo Facetti, and with 'Chico' he also drove an excellent race in the Spa 24 Hours.

Another notable victory that year was scored by de

Andrea de Adamich two-wheeling his way around Snetterton, heading for victory in the British round of the 1966 European Touring Car Championship (top). The wheel-waving cornering of these Alfas was to become familiar on circuits throughout Europe. Spartaco Dini was another GTA stalwart, here on the Cesana-Sestrières hillclimb in 1966 (centre). Jean Rolland at Cannes with his 1966 Alpine Rally winning GTA in pristine condition (bottom).

Toine Hezemans in a 1750 GTAm (left) leads the championship field away at Brno in Czechoslovakia in 1970. The 2000 GTAm had a similar specification to the 1750 GTAm. This one (below left), driven by Facetti at Jarama late in 1971, has extensions to its wheel arch extensions, to accommodate even fatter tyres.

Engine compartment of the GTA SA, the *Sovralimentata* (supercharged) GTA. The two Alfa-made centrifugal superchargers on the left were driven from a chain-drive hydraulic pump via turbines, spinning at up to 100,000rpm. The two twin-choke carburettors are between the blowers.

Adamich and Picchi in the Nürburgring 6 Hours, Larrousse won two races, and the team prize at Spa fell to Alfa Romeo. The only disappointment was that while Hezemans was clearly champion, BMW narrowly beat Alfa Romeo for marque honours.

In 1971 Hezemans had a hand in all the important race victories scored with the 2000 GTAm, driving solo at Monza, Brno and Zandvoort, with Facetti at Spa and with van Lennep at the Nürburgring and Paul Ricard. The only other top-three placing for a 2000 GTAm was achieved by Harold Ertl at Monza.

Beyond this there were hillclimb placings, Dini's third at Mont Ventoux proving the best for a GTAm, equalled by Rosselli's third with a GTAJ at Cesana-Sestrières. The

GTA 1300s at Zandvoort in 1972 (bottom), when these cars brought Alfa its last championship title in that phase of saloon car racing. Many more victories were to follow over 20 years later. Scuderia del Portello GTAs prepared for an FIA Historic Championship race at Silverstone in 1992 (left): these quick cars more than confirmed the GTA's reputation...

best Alfa placings on those important European hills in 1971 were scored with the 33-3.

GTAm driver Rosselli was only sixth in the final touring car championship points table for 1971. BMW and Ford were formidable opponents on the circuits, Capri driver Dieter Glemser becoming overall champion from Picchi and Hezemans, who maintained the Alfa record of winning the Monza series opener. Picchi's success in the 1300cc class meant that Alfa Romeo won the manufacturers' title. The GTAJ delivered the goods again in 1972, with the Divisional championship.

As with the 1570cc unit, the 1290cc engine had been tested in four-valve form by Autodelta, and a weight reduction programme was considered, but there was little point in extensive development work because the 1300cc class expired at the end of the 1972 season. Some GTAJs were still run independently in the 2-litre class into the mid-1970s, contributing odd points to Alfa's distant third place in this ETC class in 1974. Sixth place for a GTAm at Vallelunga was the best overall finish in the series.

In 1973 the 2000 GTAm was outclassed by the larger-engined BMWs and Fords, but the cars still picked up points and gave the Escorts a good run before finishing second in the 2-litre class. That year Autodelta also tried the 16-valve Alfetta in odd races – a sure sign that the coupé's racing days were numbered.

But two decades later the coupés became equally familiar on European circuits when they were joined by related Alfa Romeo saloons in historic events. They were seen in races from club level to internationals, the Scuderia del Portello cars being outstanding. The marque was numerically strong in the FIA European Challenge for Historic Touring Cars, for example when a dozen Giulia Sprints and GTAs came to the grid for the 1994 Silverstone round. Alfa's entrants were sometimes criticised for being 'too professional', but that hardly detracted from the sight of these cars lifting inside front wheels in corners just as high as they ever did...

THE LATE SPIDERS

Round tail and square tail. After 1970 Spiders look much crisper with the cut-off stern, and most enthusiasts agree **that the early Duetto tail is less appealing. From the doors forward, however, the styling was basically unchanged.**

During the late 1950s, through the mid-life period of the Giulietta Spider, Pininfarina explored Alfa two-seater themes in a series of show cars. In retrospect these tended to be flashy, for example in their fins or in excessive use of Perspex, or in unattractive combinations of angles and flowing lines as in the first two Superflow cars. Scalloped sides, noses forming a wedge in profile and two seats were common features. By 1961-62 a feasible shape was emerging in the Giulietta Spider Speciale Aerodinamica and Superfast III.

All these styling exercises led towards the production model that was introduced at the 1966 Geneva Motor Show as the new Giulia Spider, although later that year it was renamed Duetto. This bland name, with no link to Alfa Romeo or Pininfarina tradition, was decided by a

First of the Pininfarina studies, Superflow 1 of 1956, now looks an ancient vision of the future. Perspex 'bodywork' enclosed the front wheels and lights, and a large glasshouse **extended back from the cockpit between those fins – but that scalloped effect along the flanks was to be carried forward, becoming a feature of the production Duetto 10 years later.**

Pininfarina's inspiration for the Duetto included a sequence of concept cars. Superflow 2 appeared at the 1956 Paris Motor Show, with the scalloped sides that were a recurring feature, and fins that mercifully were not (left). The Spider Super Sport, or Tre S, was shown in 1959, with embyronic fairings behind the seats (below left). A Giulietta SS was the basis of the Spider Speciale Aerodinamica, here at the 1961 Turin Show (below): it had pop-up headlights and a large retractable rear window, but it is clearly a forerunner of the Duetto.

competition attracting more than 140,000 entries and won by one Guidobaldi Trionfi of Brescia, who collected a Duetto as his prize. Duetto signified a two-seater with a twin-cam engine, but the name only applied to the first 1.6-litre version of the car. It was not really accepted, and some still referred to the car as the Giulia Spider or sometimes the Spider Duetto.

Even the publicity generated by the naming was presumably welcomed by Alfa Romeo, for the new model's reception was lukewarm. 'Something more than the boulevard brougham that its make-up suggests,' was one press comment which damned with faint praise. Some of the criticism was almost dismissive, which proves that motoring journalists' judgements can be fallible. With modifications to meet safety requirements and some very mild updating, the Spider's Pininfarina lines were to live longer than most production models.

Mechanically the open sports cars followed the make-up of the Giulia, with the proven double wishbone front

suspension and live axle with trailing arms at the rear, the twin overhead camshaft 1570cc engine in its most powerful (109bhp) 1966 form, the excellent five-speed gearbox which was still a rarity, and disc brakes all round. The wheelbase was almost five inches shorter than the Giulia's, and handling was good, even though the open car was more than six inches longer than the coupé, resulting in considerable overhang front and rear.

The prominent groove along the flanks apparently played an aerodynamic role, but really this was a styling feature. The undercut nose had a 'reverse-angle' Alfa shield grille centre piece, and the headlights were faired into the wings except where regulations did not allow this – most cars for North America had exposed headlights. The cowled headlights were certainly preferable to the pop-up lights of the early-1960s show cars. There was the familiar problem of a front number plate appearing to be an afterthought in most countries, and the slender bumper was so close to the bodywork

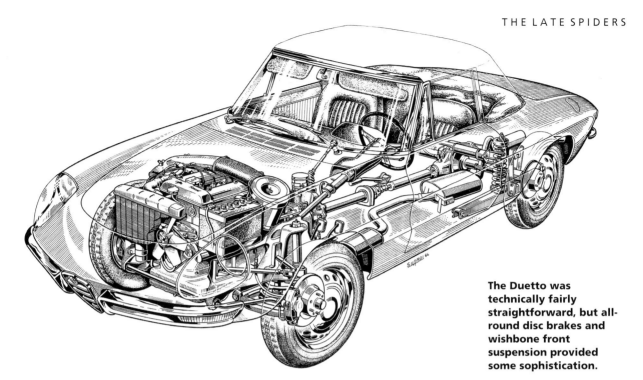

The Duetto was technically fairly straightforward, but all-round disc brakes and wishbone front suspension provided some sophistication.

that the whole nose of the car was vulnerable to minor knock damage.

The front-hinged bonnet gave reasonable access to a fairly full engine compartment, while the front-hinged boot lid enclosed a shallow boot with the spare wheel beneath it. By sports car standards there was a generous volume of luggage space.

The cockpit was neat but its trim was spartan – but then rubber floor coverings were sensible in a car of this type. Despite their shiny leatherette appearance, the seats

were generally good, although the driving position still seemed designed for the 'long arms, short legs' physique. A little more rearward seat movement would have eased this but at the cost of the trimmed rear space, which was shaped to form seats that might have been useful for very small and tolerant children, and was certainly useful for luggage.

The hand fell naturally to the gear lever, the handbrake lever on the early Duetto looked impressive, and the parking brake on this Alfa was effective. The

Familiar photograph of Alfa Romeo President Giuseppe Luraghi handing the keys of a Duetto to Guidobaldi Trionfi, winner of a name-the-car competition.

Duetto hard-top in the Alps. As with all the Spider *capote* options, this was a nicely integrated design. A 1966 Duetto (facing page, above) and a 1968 1300 Junior (facing page, below), showing minor differences in tail styling, in the front bumpers, in the faired headlights of the Duetto, and in the head restraints on the Junior's seats.

three spokes of the steering wheel incorporated horn 'buttons', and there was a single indicator stalk. Main instruments, seen through the top segment of the wheel, were a large rev counter and a matching speedometer, while secondary dials for water temperature, oil pressure and fuel were centrally mounted and angled towards the driver. There was a lockable glove compartment but no door pockets. The doors were thick, so although the Duetto was 2in (5cm) wider than the coupé, internally at shoulder level the gain was just 0.25in (0.6cm). There was the familiar ash tray/cigarette lighter on the tunnel behind the gear lever.

The soft-top was easy to raise and lower – genuinely a one-person, one-minute job – and when erect it was very effective, although unlike the optional hard-top it restricted rear three-quarter visibility. The name Duetto did not appear on the body, so there was just the Alfa badge at the nose, the company name on the boot lid and the Pininfarina 'f' on the sides behind the doors.

In most respects road testers liked the first car of the new spider generation, and its lively performance:

	Max speed	0-60 mph	Standing ¼-mile
Road & Track	113mph/182kph	11.3sec	18.5sec
Motor	111.1mph/178.7kph	11.2sec	17.7sec

Road & Track discussed the styling pros and cons, and inevitably the driving position, and was lyrical when it came to recording driving impressions: 'The overall impression is one of great responsiveness, and the feeling that the car is an extension of the driver at the controls is unmistakably clear. The steering is excellent – light, accurate and among the best we've encountered in any car.' *Motor* found 'the performance is good, the roadholding excellent and the handling superb' and in spite of a price inflated by UK import duties suggested that 'the individuality of the car, the sheer fun of driving

it and the fact that it does certain things better than many other sports cars will probably tempt some people into paying the extra'.

John Bolster pointed out in *Autosport* that the Duetto almost equalled the supercharged 8C 2300 of the 1930s in acceleration, and was 10mph (15kph) faster with roughly half the thirst for fuel…

A few cars were uprated with the GTA engine, and gained class wins in Italian races and hill-climbs. Later spiders were to seen in competition, but this was not their forte and they did not become prominent, however much fun they may have given their owners at the appropriate club level.

Sales were disappointing, just 6321 in 1966-67, with four more recorded later in the First Series ('*Osso di Seppia*'). The sports car was uprated at the beginning of 1968, along with the other Giulia models, to become the 1750 Spider Veloce. Other minor revisions were primarily to the suspension to reduce roll and understeer,

and there were fatter tyres on 14in wheels, and cockpit trim was improved.

Later in 1968 a Spider 1300 was introduced alongside the mechanically-similar GT 1300 Junior. This was aimed at the home market where its tax-paid price was some 25 per cent lower, and it increased a local rate of sale that had been poor throughout the short life of the Duetto (1300 Junior production overlapped the Second Series, with 7237 built between 1968-78). The 1300 Junior

The optional hard-top (left) for the Duetto gave excellent all-round visibility, and was offered in a contrasting colour or body colour. There was nothing ornate about the Duetto cockpit (below left), with its painted metal fascia, vinyl seats and rubber floor coverings. As usual the rev counter and speedometer are prominent, and the minor instruments are angled.

continued for a while in 'round-tail' form after the revised 'square-tail' Spider was introduced in 1970.

This styling facelift was by Filippo Sapino of Pininfarina. Slight changes were made to the nose, where the Alfa centre piece was squashed, becoming wider and shallower, and the bumpers and minor lights were revised, but the major change was at the rear. The long 'round tail' was amputated in favour of a flat-backed tail on Kamm lines, although apparently with no aerodynamic intention. The overall length of the Spider was reduced by 6.2in and boot space was cut from 7.5cu ft to 6.9cu ft. Conventional flat light clusters replaced those which had followed round the curve from flanks

into tail, and a more substantial rubber-faced bumper now ran right across the tail. The rake of the windscreen was increased to give a subtle aesthetic advantage, and smaller changes included conventional wipers and the neat flush door handles to replace the old protruding ones. Dual-circuit braking was also fitted.

A cockpit revamp was overdue, and while nothing was done to improve the driving position, at least left-hand drive cars now had pendant-hinged pedals. The painted metal fascia gave way to a padded vinyl dashboard with the main instruments protruding above it ahead of the steering wheel. The position of the secondary instruments was unchanged but the switches were regrouped on the centre console, below the gear lever. The lever itself seemed oddly placed, but Alfa felt that its position reduced the linkage to a minimum. The rearranged cockpit looked much better, but was still criticised on ergonomic grounds.

A 2000 Spider Veloce was introduced in 1971 as the first Second Series ('Coda Tronca') model, in parallel with the 2000 GTV, and shared the mechanical improvements. Outwardly, details of the wheels and badging distinguished it from the 1750 version.

Meanwhile, by late 1970 the Junior had gained the revised body, apart from details like the door handles, and the old fascia was retained until 1974. In 1972 it was complemented by the 1600 Junior with the 1570cc engine in 110bhp form. Claimed maximum speeds for the 1300 and 1600 were 170kph (106mph) and 185kph

A substantial facelift came with the Second Series (*Coda Tronca*) ranges. The 1300 Junior that had been introduced as a First Series (*Osso di Seppia*) model benefited from the square tail (right). This 2000 (below) shows the revised bumpers, with the number plate apparently hung on as an afterthought.

(115mph), neither confirmed by reliable independent tests and perhaps a little optimistic? However, output and performance figures were to become confused as specifications varied, for example with the 1976 1600 Junior having the 109bhp engine in most European countries, but the 102bhp Giulia Super engine in Italy. The 1300 ran until 1978, but was built in modest numbers, averaging less than 1000 a year.

The 2000 Spider Veloce outlived the GTV, and survived rumours of its imminent demise in the 1970s. Most of the changes to it were sparked by requirements in the US, where Spica fuel injection was already fitted. In 1975-76 the Spider was only a '49 State' car, excluded

from California until a catalytic converter was fitted. This came for 1977, when the engine was rated at 111bhp at 5000rpm, compared with the 'European engine' with twin Solex carburettors that produced 133bhp at 5500rpm. Emissions controls were ill-suited to the Spica mechanical fuel injection – or vice versa – and in 1982 it was replaced by a Bosch L-Jetronic system.

Road tests, by *Autocar* in 1976 and *Road & Track* in 1977, showed that the maximum speed was cut by the loss of power that came with emissions controls. Acceleration was so little affected that the figures are suspect, especially when compared with the American magazine's results with a 1982 car:

	Max speed	0-60 mph	Standing ¼-mile
Autocar	116mph/187kph	9.8sec	17.1sec
Road & Track	104mph/167kph	10.0sec	17.6sec

The American-market cars carried ponderous impact bumpers that extended the overall length from 162.2in (4120mm) to 168.8in (4287mm). The cockpit furnishings were modestly enhanced, and by the end of the decade the near-useless rear seats had given way to a useful flat surface for luggage.

By 1978 the Spider had been withdrawn from the British market because poor sales made the Type Approval process almost a luxury (and Alfa Romeo GB had a wide saloon range to establish on the market after a

Square tail – this change in the *Coda Tronca* cars really sharpened the design.

The Second Series lasted for a decade, and this 1980 1600 shows that red was not the only suitable colour.

difficult period of uncertainty compounded by fuel crises). Soon Spiders were imported privately, then Alfa dealer Bell & Colvill undertook right-hand drive conversions. Despite the high price (initially £9995, with items such as alloy wheels extra) there was a small but steady demand for these cars. Alfa Romeo GB did not approve and made it clear that the warranty was invalidated, despite the use of Alfa parts. Then early in 1990 Alfa announced its intention to sell the Spider in Britain again, with an approved right-hand drive conversion by Seaking.

Elsewhere Alfa Romeo persevered through the 1980s. Americans were offered the $14,995 Veloce with luxury equipment such as electric windows in 1982, alongside a low-price ($13,495) 'enthusiast' version with a basic equipment level and in a uniform ivory colour, even though everybody knew that red was the only proper colour for an Alfa Romeo sports car. This basic version of the Spider was run for a short while, perhaps to clear a backlog of chassis?

Road & Track tested a California-specification Veloce in 1982. Its engine had Bosch digital electronic ignition as well as L-Jetronic fuel injection, and was slightly more powerful with 115bhp at 5500rpm compared with 111bhp at 5000rpm. The test recorded an improved top speed of 110mph (177kph), 0-60mph in 11.7sec and a standing quarter-mile time of 18.3sec.

A facelift for 1983 was notable for the adoption on production cars of the chin and tail spoilers similar to

those on a Pininfarina car – the Spider Aerodinamica – shown nine years earlier (hence an 'Aerodinamica' title was applied to this Third Series). The bumpers were still necessarily large, the Alfa shield at the nose was in plastic-faced rubber, and the rear panel was matt black to complement the black rubber spoiler on the extremity of the boot lid. That matt treatment was carried through to the cockpit, where the bright trim around the instruments was eliminated.

These cast alloy wheels finish off a Second Series 2000, and they were to be seen on the next variant. Tear-drop door handles were so stylish that Ferrari adopted them as well.

This Aerodinamica looks good in black – perhaps because those rear spoilers are not so obvious – and the tan soft-top complements the body colour.

In a comparative test, *Road & Track* was not altogether kind: 'The seating position, large wood-rim steering wheel and long, high-mounted gear lever are peculiar to Alfa Romeo and the kindest way we can describe them is that it takes familiarity to appreciate them. The pedal layout is awful...' But its staff still hankered for the car, to the extent that punctuation was discarded in their verdict: 'Everything fits and works and feels good and it will smoke in 20,000 miles and a handle will fall off and the dash will crack but it will still give so much pleasure.'

The American market justified the continuing existence of the Spider and its variants. In 1985 there was the Graduate, a basic version owing its name to the 1967 movie in which Dustin Hoffman drove a Spider. It had vinyl seats and soft-top, and other economy fittings, and was $3000 cheaper than the $16,500 Veloce. But this 'low price' was substantially more than rivals such as the

The Third Series (Aerodinamica) cars of the 1980s saw a shift in emphasis towards a touring purpose. Compare the 1982 version (left) with this 1986 cockpit (below), which is much more luxurious. All the instruments are in a binnacle, there is a new padded steering wheel, minor switches are at the bottom of the centre console introduced with these cars, the choke and cigar lighter are behind the ashtray, and the seats look the part.

Honda Civic CRX, Toyota MR2, Mazda RX-7 and Pontiac Fiero GT, and the Alfa was a slower car. But it was an open car, and there was obviously strong loyalty and nostalgia appeal.

Demand for the Spider continued despite the arrival of new sports cars. From 1986 three types were still listed on the US market, all with mildly uprated 2-litre engines giving 120bhp at 5800rpm. The top version was the Quadrifoglio, with luxury equipment such as leather seats and air conditioning, and body extensions – almost skirts – below the sills and matched to the chin spoiler. There was an attractive hard-top with heated rear screen that could be fitted over the folded soft-top, and gave all-season versatility. The Veloce was still well equipped, and below it the entry-level Graduate remained.

The 'skirts' were to be tidied up. In 1990 sales speak, there were 'colour-coded bumpers blending into longer side pods, while a reshaped rear bumper and larger horizontal light clusters conform to the latest Alfa Romeo family look'. Importantly, the rear end was completely revised, and was once again attractive. The cockpit also received some attention, most noticeably in the single nacelle over the main instruments and some re-arrangement of the minor controls.

At the beginning of 1990 more technical changes were announced at the Detroit Show. They suggested that the perception of the Spider was indeed changing, from sports car to tourer. The principal new features were power-assisted steering and the option of automatic

transmission for the US market. Bosch Motronic engine management (integrated injection and ignition) was added to the Alfa variable inlet valve timing system from the Alfetta saloon. The Fourth Series Spider was listed in normal or Quadrifoglio Verde forms.

Europeans were still offered a 1.6-litre carburettor engine, rated at 102bhp or 104bhp depending on market, or a 2-litre unit giving 115bhp with fuel injection and catalyst or 128bhp with twin Webers. Two years on, as the Spider neared the end of its long life, there were

The Aerodinamica had new bumpers front and rear, a nose spoiler, a plastic representation of the traditional shield, and a prominent rear spoiler. From the mid-1980s Americans were offered this entry-level Graduate (above) – with cheap wheel trims – as well as the fully-equipped Veloce. An early Quadrifoglio Verde (right) car from 1986, the first year of production for this 2-litre Aerodinamica sub-series, recognised by its revised front spoiler and clumsy side skirts.

small improvements in acceleration, but the claimed top speed remained 190kph (118mph).

Engine changes between models in the Giulietta and Giulia ranges had always been feasible, but in the late 1980s a German Alfa dealer, Auto Neuser, went a step further in offering a conversion with a 2.6-litre V8, the erstwhile Montreal engine.

The 1990s mainstream 'new generation' cars had new seats, in leatherette with a suede-type centre panel that did not seem a good idea in a car that might be left open to rain (but there was still a full leather option). The seats were moved back a little, but not enough to be noticeable. Refinements included a lockable fuel filler and a remote boot release with the catch in the cockpit.

The Spider made its official return to the British market in this 2-litre form in 1990, with the interchangeable hard and soft tops as standard specification. It came as a roadster rather than as the sports car its 1970s forerunners had been, but that went to prove how the long-running design had mellowed. It

An unflattering view of the Quadrifoglio Verde. New lamp clusters and heavy bumper look ungainly, while the hard-top also falls short of Alfa's normal aesthetic excellence.

Spider on the seashore. Even with a Fourth Series car, is this a good idea? The body-colour bumpers and door mirrors are worthwhile detail improvements.

The lights might have come from Alfa's existing stock, but they blended well – the rear styling of the last Spiders was exemplary (above). Spider for the 21st Century? The exciting car (right) that was launched in 1995.

looked good, felt good in some respects, had odd little traits like the sounds of chassis movements that were almost melodic, and still had unsettling flaws like pronounced scuttle shake. It had aged well, yet showed its age.

Towards the Millenium.............................

The last of the Giulia-derived Spiders were built in April 1993, and the possibility that there might be a successor seemed remote. But a year and a half later an exiting new Spider, and a Coupé, appeared on the Alfa Romeo stand at the Paris Motor Show prior to a full launch in 1995.

The Spider and the GTV coupé were announced with three engine choices; a four-cylinder 1970cc twin-spark four-valve unit, in 150bhp or turbocharged 202bhp forms, and a 2959cc 192bhp V6. The normally-aspirated small engine should give the Spider a top speed in the region of 210kph (130mph), and the V6 perhaps 233kph (145mph), while better aerodynamics would mean that the GTV is fractionally quicker. The bodies, so much more elegant than the SZ coupé of 1990, were the work of Alfa Romeo Style Centre and Pininfarina, under the guidance of styling director Walter da Silva. In the cockpits were echoes of the old Spiders in details such as the placing of the instruments.

The reception for these cars encouraged expectations that the Alfa Romeo range would include worthy sporting successors to the Giulietta and Giulia families well into the 21st Century…

COUPÉS AND SPIDERS TODAY

The main-line Giulietta and Giulia sporting variants were built in sufficient numbers for 1990s prices to be fairly modest. The specialised types are quite another matter, and are now very sought after. Values fluctuate and are difficult to quantify, but at least in the 1990s they have fallen to realistic levels.

A coupé tends to be worth about three-quarters of the value of an equivalent Spider, but the condition and history of an individual car, as ever, can always defy generalisations, and the price gap is slightly narrower with Giuliettas. The complications of European or American specifications bear on later Spider values, 'American' cars for too long having had the drawbacks of less power and inferior handling that resulted from their raised ride height and softer suspension, but body condition can be better. A mid-1960s GTC cabriolet could equal the value of a good Spider because of its scarcity.

A GTA would be at least twice as expensive assuming it was in good condition, an SS might be bracketed with an Aston Martin DB2/4 or a Porsche 911RS in terms of value, while a further factor of three might be applied to a TZ in the rare event of one coming on the market. But the competition-oriented cars such as the GTA are specialised vehicles and have to be approached as such.

Putting the exotic models to one side, the coupés and spiders can also be realistic classics. The Giuliettas are perhaps a little fragile but the later cars are very usable. An engine in good condition is willing and strong, and the handling is always enjoyable and forgiving, although coupés obviously benefit from greater rigidity. The coupés are not claustrophobic and the Spiders have great appeal, both visually and in character. Except for those Spiders with add-ons, they are pretty cars, perhaps most eye-catching in red, and they are readily available with the back-up of specialist clubs and dealers. But they are more sophisticated and complex than most contemporary British sports cars, Duetto versions present some parts problems, and the cars which become available have almost certainly spent at least some of their lives being driven enthusiastically…

Inevitably all these cars are becoming rarer, and the rust problems which are so severe with Pininfarina's spiders have led enthusiasts and dealers in northern European countries to look to the south-western states of the USA for cars. Steps have to be taken to combat the threat of rust in a car brought into a humid climate, which may mean stripping down to the metal, and there could also be the temptation to restore the performance that was sacrificed in some 'American' cars, especially those with the 1750 engine which is perhaps the most highly regarded.

Susceptibility to rust means that inspections of chassis and body have to be an even greater priority with these Alfas than with most other classics. Every part has to be regarded as suspect, not just the mud traps in the wings, the edges of pressings and joints between panels, junctions between bodywork and trim, and the holes where accessories are mounted. The sills, the floorpan (especially if a spider soft-top has leaked), the floor of the boot (the battery was in the boot of the Giulietta), the Giulia spare wheel well, structural members (especially box sections that can create hidden areas), doors showing rust on the underside or dropping from A posts, cracks in areas such as the rear quarters, blocked drainage holes – the check list seems endless. Pininfarina Spiders seem to be particularly vulnerable because paint application and anti-rust treatment was minimal on hidden surfaces, so these cars consequently rust from within…

The best car to buy is one that has been restored professionally, by a specialist familiar with the corrosion tendencies of these cars and the steps required to combat them. The fact that the cost of major body restoration can exceed the value of a finished car adds to the wisdom of buying the best available. Specialists will know of panel availability and, apart from 'round-tail' spiders, this is generally good for the cars dating from the last quarter of a century. However, the likes of a 35-year-old Giulietta will require the services of a specialist making reproduction panels to original patterns.

Interior fittings were not always of the highest quality, and some parts may have suffered as much in hot climates as in cool humid ones. Some trim for most cars is no

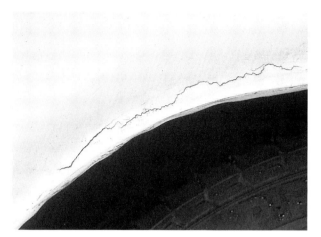

Trouble-spots on a Duetto. Jacking point filled with mud and pushed up into a sill weakened by rust (above left). Wheel arch lips are vulnerable, and sometimes badly repaired with filler (above). Duetto tail is a restoration problem because new panels are unobtainable (left): lower regions can rust extensively, while bumper can be knocked into bodywork.

longer available except possibly in service specialists' or enthusiasts' hoards, which should be known to clubs. Reproduction seats, carpets and other major items are available, but replacement of detail fittings can be very difficult, and Spider soft-tops have to be specially made.

Provided a careful maintenance regime has been adhered to, the twin-cam engines are very reliable and durable. Oil and filters should be changed every 3000 miles (5000km) and anti-freeze used conscientiously, for its corrosion-inhibiting qualities as much as for guarding against frost, since the combination of a light alloy block and iron liners makes for galvanic corrosion. Some owners have even gone so far as to use distilled water as coolant. Oil and water leaks can be signs that all is not well, with the cylinder heads and gaskets being suspect

areas, but oil droplets are acceptable, as an alloy engine tends to expand and contract when it warms up and cools down. Generally, the early (750 series) engines and parts for them are difficult to find, and parts from later units will not necessarily be interchangeable. The conversion of engines built to comply with US emissions regulations, especially those with the Spica fuel injection system, is not simple. Electric failures have been known, and Marelli components in Giulietta days did not have a high reputation although later Bosch equipment has proved to be more reliable.

In earlier cars, the gearboxes were known for weak synchromesh, especially on second gear, and wear can lead to expensive work. Fifth and reverse gear could jump out if selector rods or forks were bent. Transplants

Twin-cam Alfas in competition use today. A Giulietta Sprint being hustled at Donington (right), and an historic line-up of TZs at Laguna Seca, with some recently inflicted injuries. Autodelta sometimes ran a car with a white nose in the 1960s for ease of identification, but usually on T33s rather than on TZs.

are possible, and as an example a 101 series 'box might be used instead of an irreplaceable 750 series 'box. Clutches are also weak, with lives that reflect an owner's driving habits, for they do not take kindly to abuse. The rear axle was always rugged before the limited slip differential was introduced, first as an option on the 1750s.

Suspension condition will also reflect use and maintenance, and defects will show in handling. On a sound car this should be crisp and responsive, while the steering should be quick and have positive feedback. Brakes on this type of car tend to be used hard; bear in mind that the drums of Giuliettas can warp and discs can be damaged if pads have been allowed to wear through. Later ATE discs have higher ratings than the original Dunlop discs. The master cylinder is exposed to moisture and road dirt under the cars, and can be expensive to

replace. Once dual-circuit brakes were introduced on the right-hand drive 1750, twin servoes were fitted and replacements for these can be costly.

But the negative points should not be laboured because these cars are generally strong and well engineered, whatever the uninitiated may say to the contrary. As long as a car is treated carefully to avoid the threat of corrosion, the reward is a totally usable classic, and that cannot be said for a lot of more precious cars…

APPENDIX

Production ....

With a long-lived and diverse line of cars, it is hardly surprising that published lists of production numbers do not tally in every detail. As far as possible, this list has been checked with the Centro Documentazione Storica Alfa Romeo, but some puzzles remain. Taking the GTA as an example, some Italian sources faithfully give a figure of 500, one suspects because that was the number required for homologation, and even the official 493 may not be correct if the ten GTA SAs are shown separately. Similarly it has not been possible to confirm that the 1000 GTCs were extra to the Giulia Sprint GT total...

Technical specifications ....

Details are given for each principal model, with variations for 'sub-models'. However, quite apart from the nature of these Alfa Romeos, data such as weights could change as minor revisions were made during production. Data for the competition models is naturally representative.

Giulietta Sprint and Spider 1300
Engine In-line four-cylinder **Construction** Aluminium block and head **Crankshaft** Five-bearing **Bore × stroke** 74mm × 75mm (2.913in × 2.953in) **Capacity** 1290cc (78.69cu in) **Valves** dohc **Compression ratio** 8.1:1 **Fuel system** Solex 35 APAI-G carburettor **Maximum power** 65bhp at 6100rpm to 80bhp at 6300rpm (see text) **Maximum torque** 79.5lbft at 4000rpm **Transmission** Four-speed manual **Final drive ratio** 4.55:1 **Brakes** Drum (front disc, 1954) **Front suspension** Independent by wishbones, coil springs, telescopic dampers, anti-roll bar **Rear suspension** Live axle, trailing arms, coil springs, telescopic dampers **Steering** Worm and roller **Wheels and tyres** 4½J, 155-15 **Overall length** Sprint, 156.5in (3975mm); Spider, 152in (3861mm) **Overall width** Sprint, 60.5in (1537mm); Spider, 61in (1550mm) **Overall height** Sprint, 52in (1321mm); Spider, 52.6in (1336mm) **Wheelbase** Sprint 93.7in (2380mm); Spider, 86.7in (2200mm) **Front track** 50.9in (1292mm) **Rear track** 50in (1270mm) **Dry weight** Sprint, 1995lb (905kg); Spider, 1951lb (885kg)

Giulietta Sprint Veloce and Spider Veloce 1300
As Sprint and Spider except: **Compression ratio** 9.1:1 **Fuel system** Two Weber 40 DCO3 carburettors **Maximum power** 90bhp at 6500rpm **Maximum torque** 86.8lbft at 4500rpm **Final drive ratio** 4.1:1 **Overall length** Spider from 1959, 153.9in (3910mm) **Wheelbase** Spider from 1959, 88.6in (2250mm)

Production figures

Model	Years	Production
Giulietta Sprint	1954-62	24084
Spider	1955-58	14300
Sprint Veloce	1956-59	3058
Spider Veloce	1956-62	2907
SS	1960-61	1366
SZ	1960-62	210
Giulia Sprint	1962-64	7107
Spider	1962-65	9250
Spider Veloce	1964-66	1091
SS	1963-66	1400
TZ/TZ2	1963-67	124
Sprint GT	1963-66	21542
GTC	1963-66	1000
GTA	1965-67	394
Duetto	1966-67	6325
4R	1966-68	92
Giulia GTA SA	1967-68	10
1750 GTV	1967-72	44265
1750 Spider Veloce	1967-72	8699
Giulia GTA Junior	1968-72	492
GT 1300 Junior	1968-72	91964
Spider 1300 Junior	1968-78	7237
Spider 1600 Junior	1972-81	4848
Junior Z 1300	1969-72	1108
1750 GTAm/2000 GTAm	1970-71	40
Junior Z 1600	1972-75	402
2000 GTV	1971-77	37379
2000 Spider Veloce	1971-82	38379
GT 1600 Junior	1972-76	4495
Spider 1.6	1982-89	5400
Spider 2.0 QV	1983-89	2598
Spider 1.6 'new generation' (S4)	1990-93	2951
Spider 2.0 'new generation' (S4)	1990-93	18456

Giulietta SS

As Giulietta Sprint Veloce and Spider Veloce except: **Compression ratio** 9.5:1 **Maximum power** 100bhp at 6500rpm **Maximum torque** 96.2lb ft at 4500rpm **Transmission** Five-speed manual **Overall length** 167in (4242mm) **Overall width** 65.3in (1659mm) **Overall height** 48.8in (1240mm) **Front track** 50.6in (1286mm) **Dry weight** 2094lb (950kg)

SZ

As Giulietta SS except: **Compression ratio** 9.7:1 **Maximum power** 118bhp at 6500rpm **Maximum torque** 96lb ft at 4500rpm **Overall length** 151.5in (3848mm) **Overall width** 60.2in (1529mm) **Overall height** 48.5in (1232mm) **Unladen weight** 1890lb (857kg)

Giulia Sprint and Spider

As Giulietta Sprint and Spider except: **Bore × stroke** 78mm × 82mm (3.07in × 3.23in) **Capacity** 1570cc (95.8cu in) **Compression ratio** 9.1:1 **Fuel system** Weber carburettor, later Solex 32 PA1A **Maximum power** 92bhp at 6200rpm **Transmission** Five-speed manual **Final drive ratio** 5.125:1 **Brakes** Disc front, drum rear **Dimensions** Spider as Spider Veloce 1300 **Unladen weight** Sprint 1993lb (905kg); Spider, 1950lb (885kg)

Giulia Spider Veloce

As Giulia Sprint and Spider except: **Compression ratio** 9.7:1 **Fuel system** Two Weber 40 DCOE 2 carburettors **Maximum power** 112bhp at 6500rpm **Maximum torque** 96lb ft at 4500rpm **Final drive ratio** 4.555:1

Giulia SS

As Giulietta SS except: **Bore × stroke** 78mm × 82mm (3.07in × 3.23in) **Capacity** 1570cc (95.8cu in) **Compression ratio** 9.7:1 **Fuel system** Two Weber 40 DCOE 2 carburettors **Maximum power** 112bhp at 6500rpm **Maximum torque** 98.3lb ft at 4200rpm. **Brakes** Disc front and rear **Overall height** 50.4in (1280mm)

Giulia TZ

As Giulia SS except: **Compression ratio** Up to 11.4:1 **Maximum power** Up to 170bhp (see text) **Rear suspension** Independent, by wishbones with axles as upper links, coil springs, shock absorbers, anti-roll bar **Overall length** 155.5in (3950mm) **Overall width** 59.4in (1510mm) **Overall height** 47.2in (1210mm) **Wheelbase** 86.6in (2211mm) **Track, front and rear** 51.2in (1300mm) **Unladen weight** 1433lb (650kg)

Giulia Sprint GT

Engine In-line four-cylinder **Construction** Aluminium block and head **Crankshaft** Five-bearing **Bore × stroke** 78mm × 82mm (3.07in × 3.23in) **Capacity** 1570cc (95.8cu in) **Valves** dohc **Compression ratio** 9.01:1 **Fuel system** Two Weber 40 DCOE 4 carburettors **Maximum power** 106bhp at 6000rpm **Maximum torque** 103lb ft at 3000rpm **Transmission** Five-speed manual **Final drive ratio** 4.555:1 **Brakes** Disc **Front suspension** Independent by wishbones, coil springs, telescopic dampers, anti-roll bar **Rear suspension** Live axle, trailing arms, T-arm, coil springs, telescopic dampers **Steering** Worm and roller, or recirculating ball **Wheels and tyres** 4½J, 155-15 **Overall length** 161in (4088mm) **Overall width** 62.2in (1580mm) **Overall height** 51.7in (1315mm) **Wheelbase** 92.5in (2350mm) **Front track** 51.5in (1310mm) **Rear track** 50in (1270mm) **Unladen weight** 2128lb (965kg)

GTC

As Giulia Sprint GT except: **Weight** 2100lb (950kg)

GTA

Engine In-line four-cylinder **Construction** Aluminium block and head **Crankshaft** Five-bearing **Bore × stroke** 78mm × 82mm (3.07in

× 3.23in) **Capacity** 1570cc (95.8cu in) **Compression ratio** 9.7:1 to 10.5:1 **Fuel system** Two Weber 45 DCOE 14 carburettors **Maximum power** 115bhp at 6000rpm to 170bhp at 7500rpm **Maximum torque** 119lb ft to 148lb ft at 5500rpm **Transmission** Five-speed manual, limited-slip differential **Final drive ratio** 4.555:1 **Brakes** Disc front and rear **Front suspension** Independent by wishbones, coil springs, telescopic dampers, anti-roll bar **Rear suspension** Live axle, trailing arms, Panhard rod, coil springs, telescopic dampers **Steering** Worm and roller or recirculating ball **Wheels and tyres** 4½J, 155HR-15 **Overall length** 160.5in (4080mm) **Overall width** 62.2in (1580mm) **Overall height** 51.8in (1315mm) **Wheelbase** 92.5in (2350mm) **Front track** 51.6in (1310mm) **Rear track** 50in (1270mm) **Unladen weight** 1808lb (820kg), see text

Duetto

As Giulia Sprint GT except: **Maximum power** 109bhp at 6000rpm **Overall length** 167.3in (4250mm) **Overall width** 64.2in (1630mm) **Overall height** 50.8in (1290mm) **Wheelbase** 88.6in (2250mm) **Weight** 2180lb (988kg)

GTA SA

As GTA except: **Compression ratio** 10.5:1 **Fuel system** Two carburettors, two centrifugal superchargers **Maximum power** 200bhp at 7500rpm **Front track** 52.1in (1324mm) **Rear track** 50.1in (1274mm) **Unladen weight** 1718lb (780kg)

GTA 1300 Junior (GTAJ)

As GTA except: **Bore × stroke** 78mm × 67.5mm (3.07in × 2.657in) **Capacity** 1290cc (78.69cu in) **Compression ratio** 9.0:1 **Fuel system** Two carburettors or Spica fuel injection **Maximum power** 96bhp at 6000rpm to 165bhp at 8400rpm **Wheels and tyres** 5½J, 165-HR **Front track** 52.1in (1324mm) **Unladen weight** 1674lb (760kg)

GT 1300 Junior

As Giulia Sprint GT except: **Bore × stroke** 74mm × 75mm (2.913in × 2.953in) **Capacity** 1290cc (78.69cu in) **Fuel system** Two Weber 40 DCOE 28 carburettors **Maximum power** 89bhp at 6000rpm **Maximum torque** 101lb ft at 3200rpm **Rear suspension** Anti-roll bar from 1970 **Unladen weight** 2045lb (928kg); from 1970, 2183lb (990kg)

GT 1600 Junior

As GT Sprint except: **Fuel system** Two Weber 40 DCOE 27, Dell'Orto DHLA 40 or Solex C40 DDH6 carburettors **Maximum power** 110bhp at 6000rpm **Maximum torque** 115lb ft at 2800rpm **Rear suspension** Incorporates anti-roll bar **Front track** 52.1in (1323mm) **Unladen weight** 2244lb (1020kg)

1300 and 1600 Junior Z

As GT 1300 and 1600 Junior except: **Overall length** 157.5in (4000mm) **Overall width** 61in (1550mm) **Overall height** 50.4in (1280mm) **Wheelbase** 88.6in (2250mm) **Unladen weight** 2094lb (950kg)

1750 GT Veloce

As Giulia Sprint GT except: **Bore × stroke** 80mm × 88.5mm (3.15in × 3.48in) **Capacity** 1779cc (108.6cu in) **Compression ratio** 9.5:1 late cars 9.0:1 **Fuel system** Two Weber 40 DCOE 32 carburettors; US specification, Spica fuel injection **Maximum power** 122bhp at 5500rpm; late cars 188bhp at 5500rpm **Maximum torque** 137lb ft at 2900rpm **Final drive ratio** 4.1:1, US specification, 4.56:1 **Rear suspension** Incorporates anti-roll bar **Wheels and tyres** 5½J, 165-14 **Overall length** 161.4in (4100mm) **Unladen weight** 2293lb (1040kg)

1750 Spider Veloce

As 1750 GT Veloce except: **Overall length** 'Square tail' from 1970, 162.2in (4120mm) **Overall width** 64.2in (1630mm) **Overall height**